UNCOILING THE ROPES

Clare Sheridan

MWEELREA PRESS

First published in 2020 by
Mweelrea Press
Dublin, Ireland
mweelreapress@gmail.com

Amazon paperback	ISBN: 978 1 78846 162 7
Paperback	ISBN: 978 1 78846 159 7
Ebook – mobi format	ISBN: 978 1 78846 160 3
Ebook – epub format	ISBN: 978 1 78846 161 0

Produced by Kazoo Independent Publishing Services
222 Beech Park, Lucan, Co. Dublin
www.kazoopublishing.com

Kazoo Independent Publishing Services is not the publisher of this work. All rights and responsibilities pertaining to this work remain with Mweelrea Press.

Kazoo offers independent authors a full range of publishing services. For further details visit www.kazoopublishing.com

Front cover photo: *Climbing in the Bugaboos, British Columbia.*
Back cover photo: *Among the Chamonix Aiguilles.*

Cover design by Oscar Torrans

Printed in the EU

UNCOILING THE ROPES

For Calvin

Prologue

Himalayas, 1977

I'm getting sunburnt under my chin. Damn. I'll have to stop now and take off this monster rucksack to get the cream out. Stupid of me to forget how the sun reflects back up off the snow and how this crystal-clear Himalayan light searches out every strip of exposed skin to blister and burn.

There are five of us plodding steadily along the side of a huge glacier. We each walk at our own pace, and now that we've become separated I have the jumbled landscape of rocks and scree to myself. Two of my companions, Calvin Torrans and Anthony Latham, are somewhere up ahead, and there's no sign yet of the other pair, Emmett Goulding and Joss Lynam.

I heft the heavy pack frame off my shoulders and balance it on my hip before letting it slide on down to the ground; it wouldn't do to hurt my back right at the start of the expedition. This might be a good time too to nip behind a big boulder, seeing that I'm on my own. I lean the rucksack against a stone and step towards the boulder – but I never make it. Suddenly I'm swaying and then teetering as the dust and gravel beneath my feet open wide. I feel myself lurch and drop. And then I disappear from the face of the earth.

I fall through a rush of cold air and jolt to a halt between smooth green-tinged walls of glass. I'm inside the glacier. The stony ground I've been walking on has abruptly unmasked itself as treacherous crevassed ice. The surface, delicate enough to give way under a footfall, has been cloaking a gaping crack, a crack that with a quiet whoosh has just swallowed the big boulder and me.

What stopped me falling? There's no sign now of the boulder, and I don't dare breathe as I strain to see what checked my plunge. I'm suspended, caught between two walls of ice that sweep down to nightmare depths. One foot hangs free, but the heel of the other has caught on something. Something small. I peer down. It's a tiny ice ledge, and I realise with horror that this one little bump is all that is holding me above the drop.

My stomach shrinks as I lock every muscle. If I don't control my panic I'll dislodge myself. The crevasse, a great vertical slit in the glacier, has walls that flare and narrow, wide enough in places to devour a boulder but tight enough elsewhere to trap a human body, almost.

Where I've fallen I've hit a narrowing, a slot twice as wide as myself, and I'm wedged loosely across it, one elbow jammed against the opposite wall. The cold is seeping into that elbow, and it will soon begin to cramp, but I don't dare move. If I put my palm on the ice to push myself upright, I'll tilt my heel off the bump and vanish for ever.

This was the summer of my twenty-fourth birthday, and I was in Kashmir, India, to climb virgin Himalayan peaks. We had been carrying loads to establish a high camp below our first unclimbed mountain. It rose in a near perfect triangle of rock and snow at the head of the glacier in front of us. Our rucksacks were heavy with food supplies, climbing equipment and camping gear, and they dragged at our shoulders and deadened our backs. We were at well over 4,000 metres, and the air was thin, but I was very happy to be there and content with my progress so far. I was carrying as much as the men, and it was manageable as long as I kept to a slow steady pace.

We had stayed at the edge of the glacier, on the moraine, the ridge of rubbly debris that had been pushed to the side by the slow-moving ice. If we went out onto the glacier proper we'd have to rope up because of the threat of crevasses under the snowy surface, so it was better to stay at the side where everyone could walk independently.

We had trudged along, our minds elsewhere as we zigzagged

between boulders and over mounds of scree, struggling to keep our balance on wobbling stones and collapsing snow patches. The terrain was like a builder's waste tip, and there was no clue that the rocks and gravel were just a coating, a dusty veneer that veiled the jaws of crevasses. And now I had broken through the veneer and was trapped below the surface.

I could die. *No, no*, I thought, *surely the others will rescue me*. But what if I fell further? A fall to the bottom of the crevasse would probably kill me – it could be a further drop of 50 metres or more. And what if I was just injured? How would they ever get me out? Calvin would be the one who'd come down looking for me. Of course it would be Calvin, my climbing partner and beloved boyfriend.

The others would lower him carefully and he'd spin around slowly at the end of the rope, the beam of his head torch glancing off the ice walls. Would they have enough rope? Would he get to where I'd be lying, crumpled, in the dark? And if they did manage to haul me up, injured, what then? We were alone on the glacier and there was no rescue team to call on. The nearest phone was in the town of Kishtwar, a full week's walk away.

I calmed my breathing and tried to judge how far I'd fallen. Not far: just two or three body lengths. Was there any way I could climb out? I glanced down again and saw how the plunge below curved immediately into shadow. It would be dark below the curve, dark all the way to the bottom. *Oh, God, God*. I wasn't praying. I had no shred of belief, no hope in an Almighty, but through gritted teeth the words still came. Curses now. *Jesus! Jesus Christ! What the hell do I do now? Just wait? Wait till the ice bump breaks and I slide on down?* I was powerless.

But I wasn't dead. I could hang on here until one of the others came looking for me. How long before they missed me? It could be hours. Emmett and Joss were my best bet, but they'd have their eyes down as they negotiated the snow patches and rough ground, and they might walk right past my rucksack without noticing it. I shouted, roared, my voice the only part of me not paralysed. And then I waited and listened. Nothing. *Just take it easy. Stay calm. Shout again in a minute*.

A current of freezing air came up past my face and new waves of fear shot through me. The little bump could crumble at any moment and deliver me to the icy monsters of darkness and pain lying in wait below. I screamed and roared and held my breath to listen. Then a voice. Emmett! *Oh thank God, thank God.*

He was shouting for directions. *No, stop.* If he rushed over to my rucksack, the fragile lip of the crevasse could collapse in on top of me. He might even fall in himself. I shouted a warning, and then, taking great care not to dislodge myself, I used my free hand to take off my denim sun hat and fling it upwards. Emmett spotted the flicker of it just breaking the surface.

He edged forward on his stomach and peered cautiously into the crack. I could see his head. *Keep still, keep still. It's not over yet.* He'd get me out. Or would there be time?

'Hang on,' he yelled. 'I'll throw you a rope.' Within minutes he had anchored himself to a boulder well away from the crevasse edge and was ready to lower a loop of rope to me. Squinting, I saw it snaking down from the sunlight. *Don't rush . . . wait . . .* I grabbed it, pulled it over my head and my free shoulder and let the panic explode as I clawed wildly up the vertical ice.

Chapter 1

It all started the day the hiker came. That was the day when we first heard that people sometimes went into the mountains, just to walk. We were living in Bantry, in West Cork, where my father worked as a primary-school inspector. He was based there from 1958, when I was six, until the mid 1960s. Our house was on the outskirts of the town, just half a mile from the sea, and my sister Bairbre and I would often wander down there after school.

Newtown strand wasn't much of a place for swimming as it was just a strip of stony shore below the last field, but it was all right for a paddle on a hot day. That afternoon there were a few other children there, with their mammies, and one of them said there was a hiker on the strand. We'd have been excited to see a Yank or some other kind of foreigner, but a hiker? That was something new. We stood on the seaweed-crested high-tide mark and looked around. But there was nothing unusual, just pebbles and shells and a child pouring water into a circle of stones.

Bairbre scrambled onto an earthen bank to look into a mucky gully beyond. I followed, but then, inexplicably, I found myself alone. I swivelled round, feeling exposed now on my big tuft of sandy earth and suddenly, urgently, needing to know what a hiker was. It sounded vicious. Was it like the bogeyman who did awful things to the children he caught out after dark? Was it lurking just below me, its long hand already reaching through the fringe of grass to grab me by the leg?

Images of scaly grasping limbs overwhelmed me and I did something I'd never chosen to do before. I screamed.

Children didn't scream for attention when I was young, or if they did it was not for long as the vocal build-up to a tantrum was always cut short by the brisk sound of a parent's slap. Screams were reserved for pain or terror, and the adults who heard them listened with concern. I closed my eyes and howled until someone else's mother lifted me down. 'The hiker?' she said. 'Ah sure it's just a young man with a knapsack, probably Dutch or German. God only knows what's brought him down here.'

We never saw the hiker in the end, and as we made our way up the lane towards home, Bairbre said we'd call in to the fairy fort. She was always the one who decided what hill or hollow or stream we'd head to when we shouted to my mother that we were going 'out the fields'. She was only a year older than me but she had lots of *teaspie*, as they used to say in Bantry. Not that exuberance was much appreciated in Ireland in the 1950s, especially not in a girl.

Bairbre was the one who cycled on walls and who, when we were both still small, pulled the back off my cot to release me because she needed someone to play with. We shared a bed until our teens and a room, plus most of our experiences, until our twenties. She was always the one who planned our adventures, and she was always the boss.

The fairy fort was in a field where the grass was short and there were no cows to dirty it. It was a circle of tightly growing hazel trees that no farmer would dare cut down for fear of the wrath of the Little People who lived inside. Irish fairies, the *Sí*, were nothing like the English fairies we came across in books. English fairies were lovely. They were pretty, colourful little things who lived in flowers and liked to smile and be helpful. The *Sí* were to be feared. They were powerful creatures who took a malignant delight in interfering in human affairs.

Inside the fairy fort, the hazels were impenetrable, except at crawling level, and we bent double to scuttle through them on rabbit tracks. We didn't really believe in the fairy folk, as long as the sun was shining, but there were old people we knew who did. For them there was always more to the lie of the land than met the eye, and every lone thorn tree and oddly shaped rock had a story to tell. This made sense to Bairbre and me and added some magic to our explorations as we strayed further and further from home. We were intrigued by the local landscape long before we noticed the mountains that lay beyond it.

At teatime we told my parents about the hiker, skipping the details of my panic. My father, who knew everything, said that West Cork was a wonderful place for hiking. He said hiking was just walking in the mountains and that he'd been thinking of doing it himself, as soon as we were old enough to go with him. He had grown up among the little drumlins of land-locked Cavan and was enthralled by Bantry Bay and the Beara Peninsula that bounded it to the west. For him the purple-grey skyline of the Caha Mountains was full of promise, and he said he'd bring us walking there sometime soon.

Our first outing was the following spring. I was nine by then and Bairbre ten, and my father brought us to Gougane Barra, a valley hidden in a fold of the mountains on the Cork–Kerry border. Gougane has a beautiful lake and on its shore a tiny church, a delicate ark of light-coloured stone set amid the ridges of the rough dark hills. This had been the site of an early Christian hermitage, according to my father, and in later years the valley served as a hideout for rebels in conflict with the English crown. The whole place seemed alive with mystery when my father pushed a few fronds of damp bracken aside to show us a Mass rock. This flat stone had been used as a secret altar during the days of the Penal Laws, the ruggedness of the terrain serving to screen the fugitive priests and their people from the searching redcoats.

We didn't get very far that day in Gougane Barra. After clambering part way up a steep hill, we decided we were too tired to carry on. My father agreed that we should turn back but said we could go down by a different, more interesting, route. He brought us to the edge of a gully that cut deep into the heathery slope and told us that this had been the scene of a daring escape in 1921, during the War of Independence. IRA guerrilla leader Tom Barry had led his flying column over these mountains, at night, to avoid capture by

British troops and had come down by this very ravine. At night? We were impressed. The rocky cleft looked tricky even in daylight but my father reckoned that it shouldn't be too hard to descend. So we followed him into it, and almost immediately got stuck. It had been a hard winter, and we found ourselves in an icy three-sided chimney where we couldn't go up or down without risk to life and limb.

My father came up with a solution of sorts: he would slide down a bit and brace himself against a rock or tree root and then Bairbre and I would let go, in turn, and shoot down to crash into him. We repeated this until we got to easier ground and could scramble off to the side. Soon we were romping down the last slope, kicking up dead leaves and half-frozen moss and catching glimpses of the lake between the trees. We were in high spirits now. We had survived the ice and had a story to tell when we got home.

A few years later, my parents went on a walking tour over the mountains from Bantry to Gougane and on into Kerry. They were away for five days while a drafted-in housekeeper looked after the two of us and our little brothers, Shane and Myles. My father had sent to London for heavy leather walking boots and he and my mother had done some training walks around Bantry. The neighbours shook their heads. 'Yerra, sure what would they want to be doing that for, and he with a car at the door?'

When they got back, we half listened to the names of the valleys and mountain passes they'd walked over: Coomhola, Borlin Valley, the Priest's Leap. They'd had a great time in spite of bad weather and blisters. My mother always wore a skirt when she went walking, and white ankle socks. She had no ambition to tread on lofty peaks, but she loved the adventure of a day out, a day under the open sky, far from the reach of ordinary life. She would tell us how she and my father used to go for long walks together when they were a young courting couple in Limerick. There was one day in particular that she mentioned time and again. They'd spent it in the Glen of Aherlow, and I think it may have been one of the happiest days of her life.

But my mother's forays into the wild were numbered. She and my father had just one other walking holiday together before the growing family took all of her energies. My father continued hill walking until the end of his life and succeeded in passing his love of mountains on to each of his seven children.

Religion was an unquestioned part of our lives when we lived in Bantry. Before bedtime, we would all kneel for the ritual of the family rosary, and the only picture in each of the bedrooms was a mass-produced religious image in a dark frame. For Bairbre and me it was the Sacred Heart and his sad, sad eyes would follow us around as we moved. At home our Catholicism was always low-key, and it was left to the nuns in the local Mercy convent school to deal with the heavy doctrines of the church – the teachings on sin, guilt, purgatory, heaven and hell. This laid the groundwork for the repressive moral moulding that Bairbre and I were to encounter in our teens when we were sent away to a convent boarding school.

There was one central church message that the nuns in both convent schools were anxious to pass on to us: the female body was to be viewed negatively and needed to be carefully controlled lest it become an occasion for sin. The first hint of this came when I was ten. My teacher read us the story of Maria Goretti, the young Italian girl who had suffered martyrdom by multiple stab wounds (seventeen, we were told) rather than submit to a man and a fate worse than death. Not one of us in Sister Joseph's fourth class had any idea what that fate might be.

There were no tales of holy martyrs at home, though my father read to us constantly, even when we were old enough to zip through *Anne of Green Gables* and the Hardy Boys books on our own. Our high-ceilinged sitting room was cold and unwelcoming until the fire was lit, and then the cosiness flickered on the good mahogany sideboard and the Waterford crystal wedding presents.

Coming up to Christmas my father always bought a case of oranges and their smell warmed every corner when he settled down to read to us. I would sit on the carpet beside his armchair and listen with bated breath to the dramas of Tom Sawyer and Huck Finn, Toad of Toad Hall and the great Celtic hero, Cúchulainn. But it was the stories of Irish novelist Patricia Lynch that felt most real. Her cosy stone cabins at the edge of the bog beneath the mountains were the scattered cottages out beyond Glengarriff. And whenever we went walking in the hills, any grassy boreen or lonely sheep pen might glow, fleetingly, with a ray of her fiction.

On Good Friday, my father always brought Bairbre, Shane and me hill walking in the Caha Mountains. My mother would stay with the baby and the toddler, listening to *Woman's Hour* on BBC radio and getting the fish ready for dinner. It had to be fish, for that prime day of abstinence, and it was always just a tea-dinner.

I hated tea-dinners. A dinner was never a proper dinner if the steamy earthiness of freshly boiled potatoes wasn't rising from the table when we trooped into the kitchen. Bread, butter and tea, plus fried fish, made for cold comfort. Good Friday was the day of officially decreed misery when the hours piled up slowly to the guilt of three o'clock: the time at which Jesus had died on the cross.

We were a subdued little group as we headed up the first slopes of Sugarloaf Mountain. Walking uphill never seemed like a good idea, in spite of my father's encouraging talk of getting a second wind. Our spirits would lift as we got higher, and we'd have a last rush to the summit to prance around on the warm sandstone. Now we had all of Bantry Bay and the Beara Peninsula laid out before us. My father would point out a mountain ridge or the gleam of a lake in the distance and tell us its name, the Irish words capturing the contours and lending them mystery.

There were stories in all of these mountains. This was where the Gaelic chief O'Sullivan Beare had been defeated by the Elizabethan army in 1602. It was through the valleys below us that he had set out on his slow trek north to seek the protection of his allies in Ulster, his castle burning and his anxious people tramping miserably behind him. The sea held further romances. French ships had sailed into Bantry Bay in 1796, coming to the aid of the United Irishmen in their fight for freedom, but storms and the wily British navy had got the better of them. We never met anyone else in the mountains, but when we'd get back to the car there would always be an old farmer leaning on a gate, eager for a chat. And one of them spoke as if the French fleet had only just turned for home.

We walked, just once, to the top of Knockboy, the highest point in County Cork, but the terrain was dull and boggy, and there were no rocky outcrops to play and scramble on. We discovered that highest didn't necessarily mean best. The big mountain was Hungry Hill, the great dark whale of Beara, visible from miles away as it rose above the little coves and headlands beyond Glengarriff. It was a mountain we attempted a couple of times, but our short legs weren't up to it.

Changes in the weather often defeated us too as my father hadn't mastered the use of a compass. We'd have been hard pressed to withstand bad weather anyway, in our jumpers, slacks and wellingtons, and the raincoats that my father carried for us in his old khaki knapsack. I was always a tomboy, and as T-shirts and jeans hadn't yet crossed the Atlantic, I longed for clothes that were comfortable and tough and looked as if the wearer were ready for any adventure. I set my heart on a cowgirl's playsuit as the best compromise – I already had the guns, holsters and cowboy hat – but the suit, when my mother managed to get me one, turned out to be a flimsy decorated disappointment.

When there was no place to go and no one to play with, there was always the swing. You couldn't just buy a swing and ours was made by a carpenter who erected it at the side of the house. Once the wooden frame had been lodged solidly in the ground, an old sailor came up from the harbour to do the final job – the expert splicing of each of the ropes that held the seat.

But you could get bored with the swing, and I decided one day to climb onto the top of it. It was easy enough to clamber up the supports and go hand over hand across the main beam, but climbing up onto the top of that beam was a different sort of challenge. It took nerve. Getting from crouched to standing and then walking the few steps along it, high above the ground, with nothing to grab at but the empty air . . . Could I do it? Would I do it? What would it feel like?

I straightened up and edged along the narrow beam in my brown leather shoes, tense to my wavering fingertips. Panic hovered beside me, but I was steady enough. When I lowered off the end and dropped down onto the beaten-earth path beside the privet hedge, everything felt different. I'd stepped out of my day into something absorbing and uncertain and intense, and when I stepped back again I found that the day wasn't boring anymore. And I wasn't exactly who I used to be.

Chapter 2

Bairbre and I spent our last two years of primary school in a rural two-teacher national school outside Bantry. Inchiclough had a growing reputation for winning county-council scholarships, and my father saw it as a promising alternative to what he knew to be the limited educational offerings of the Mercy convent school in the town. Inchiclough was three miles from our house, and we walked and later cycled the narrow roads where the trees met overhead and cars were rare. We dawdled eating sorrel leaves and hawthorn 'bread and butter' and picking at melted tar, but we couldn't relax. School was often a scary place, even for the inspector's daughters.

In the early 1960s, free secondary education hadn't come in yet, and winning a scholarship to secondary school was a serious business, particularly for our classmates who were the children of impoverished small farmers. Out of the twenty or so pupils that he taught, the master gave our scholarship group of five most of his attention every day. His approach included ridicule, sarcasm and corporal punishment – all acceptable methods of maintaining pupil motivation and classroom control at the time.

We all got the scholarship, and for Bairbre and me it meant that our parents could afford to send us away to boarding school. Going away to school was a very exciting prospect as we had read a lot about boarding schools in our comics, *Bunty*, *Judy* and *Diana*, and in Enid Blyton's St Clare's novels. We knew all about midnight feasts and admirable head girls, though there were no nuns in any of those stories.

Laurel Hill in Limerick had a reputation for being one of the top girls' schools in the country. It was run by the Faithful Companions of Jesus, originally a French order, and the nuns prided themselves not only on their academic results but also on the calibre of the young ladies they turned out.

We learned a lot in our first half-term. We learned that our sing-song West Cork accents were ridiculous; that girls whose mothers were past pupils were more cherishable; that you used a knife and a fork to eat apples, oranges and bananas; and that causing a spill on the starched tablecloth in the refectory showed weakness of character. It was hard to go back after Hallowe'en.

The school was near the centre of Limerick city, and we were forbidden to leave the grounds. This was a big change for a couple of youngsters who had been used to roaming the countryside at will. We were to spend much of the following five years indoors. From the dormitory windows you could look out over the gardens, the tennis courts and the hockey fields, and the avenue of glorious beech trees that looped down to the boundary wall. Beyond the wall were the great concrete silos of Ranks flour mill and then the docks on the Shannon Estuary. Beyond the river, the suburbs of Limerick stretched away towards a string of modest hills on the Limerick–Clare border, hills that had none of the tempting wildness of the Caha Mountains.

In one of his weekly letters my father mentioned that he had made another attempt at Hungry Hill.

> *11 February 1965*
>
> On Saturday last I set off with Shane and the Riordan brothers to attempt the ascent of Hungry Hill. But it will still be there unconquered when you come home. A local sheep farmer strongly advised us not to attempt it. How right he was: the entire mountainside was cased in ice and only a skilled alpine climber could have got to the top – not to speak of coming down again.

Hungry Hill? And with the neighbouring boys instead of us? This sort of dispatch from the home front was very unsettling.

We never did make it to the top of Hungry Hill with my father. He got a promotion at work soon after that, and within months we had moved to Dublin. His heart continued to ache for those lost Beara landscapes for many a long year afterwards

In Laurel Hill the moral imperative was to act like a lady at all times. This involved a far more complicated framework of right and wrong than the one overseen by the image of the Sacred Heart at home. Mother Dympna, the nun charged with making young ladies of us, was tireless in correcting the way we stood, sat, walked, spoke and ate. Her exhortations were constant: 'Shoulders back and heads up!' 'Knees, legs, feet together!' and her vivid interdiction of taking a drink while eating: 'Don't make a pudding in your mouth!'

The ideal of the young lady was an amalgamation of snobbishness, religion and straightforward Victorian repression. Bairbre and I felt an immediate and instinctive distrust of every aspect of it. It was full of prohibitions and there was no place in it for the adventurous activities that we loved. We were told that we should aspire to be like Mary, the eternal Virgin, of whom there were various plaster statues around the school. With her blank even features and downcast eyes, she was of little interest – until you saw her feet. The delicate bare feet, just visible beneath the flowing blue and white robes, were planted solidly on the small ugly head of the serpent. This was the Virgin's mighty power, and it could be ours too if we sought her help: the power to resist temptation, the power to say no.

For the nuns, lifelong virginity was a woman's highest calling, if she were privileged enough to have a vocation. How could it not be? You were preserving yourself as a bride for Christ. Of course other women would make different choices because children had to be brought into this world and married couples would do what they had to do, but that was best not thought about and certainly not talked about.

The Virgin Mary, with her spotless soul and submissive character, was the perfect role model for Catholic girls. Her outstanding attribute, her virginity, was glorified beyond measure. She might be

Holy Mary Mother of God, but above all else she was the Blessed Virgin. And in the Ireland of the 1960s, where every town had a Marian shrine, Mary's perpetual virginity cast a long shadow.

The sex education provided by the school was very limited, but it came with clear warnings: we must behave modestly at all times; we must avoid occasions for sin; and we must ensure that intimacy before marriage never went beyond chaste kisses. As voracious readers, Bairbre and I, and our friends, educated ourselves about sex, and when my mother gave us the Catholic Truth Society pamphlet *My Dear Daughter* by Angela MacNamara, we found that we knew it all already. Bairbre passed the pamphlet on to another girl, but a nun spotted it and it was confiscated. Sex was shameful, and ignorance, particularly in girls, was a virtue.

We were in the same class all through secondary school – much to Bairbre's chagrin – and when we were in Fifth Year, a charismatic young nun arrived to teach us religion. We were never the same after. Sister Winifred had taught in London and came to us freshly energised by the Second Vatican Council. She presented religion as a real quest for personal meaning rather than an endless cycle of mindless rituals and devotion to the Virgin. She discussed big ideas with us and asked our opinion. Suddenly we weren't just clever, we were intelligent, and we adored her. For us she was a strong female role model, and becoming a nun began to look like a thrilling spiritual and intellectual adventure. And we weren't drawn to any compelling alternative: moving to Dublin in our teens had been a social disaster for Bairbre and me, and we hadn't yet got to know any boys.

In the Christmas tests in Sixth Year, I came first in the class in religious instruction, and by the spring of 1969 we had both decided that we had vocations to join the Faithful Companions of Jesus. Bairbre was accepted for the novitiate for the following September, but I, to my great disappointment, was told that I was too young and should wait a year.

Chapter 3

In the summer of 1968, when I turned sixteen, Bairbre and I headed off with our bicycles on our first independent holiday. Our parents didn't object; they were always more encouraging than protective. We got the train to Sligo and spent a couple of weeks cycling around Donegal and staying in An Óige youth hostels before crossing the border into Northern Ireland.

One wild day in Donegal, we wasted hours sheltering behind turf ricks from the heavy squalls and then realised we wouldn't make it to the new hostel below Errigal mountain. Deciding we'd better find somewhere else to stay, we stopped at the next farmhouse we came to. An elderly woman answered the door. When we asked if we could sleep in her barn, she exclaimed, 'Oh no, we'll have none of your sort around here. I have two men in the house!'

We were horrified! What did she take us for? We slunk away, mortally embarrassed. A few miles further on we found an abandoned cottage well off the road and spent the night there. The skeleton roof beams were open to the sky, and the plaster-backed wallpaper hung down in damp strips from the ruined walls. We had no sleeping bags and spent a cold sleepless night sitting on mouldy planks with our thin sheet bags pulled around our shoulders.

Our plan, all worked out by Bairbre, brought us in a loop around the north-west coast and over into Derry. We hadn't been in the North before and noted with interest the unfamiliar tidiness of the farms and the eye-catching red of the postboxes and telephone booths. The signposts were all in English only and looked flat and one-dimensional, sheared as they were from their roots. The real place names, *Doire*, *Tír Eoghain*, *Fir Manach*, came to us from school history and geography as we cycled by. We knew little about the North other than that it was still under British rule and that the people who lived there were mainly Protestant. And that you could buy sweets like Opal Fruits that you couldn't get at home.

When we were south of Omagh I got a puncture, and we discovered that we'd lost our repair kit somewhere along the way. We called to a house and explained our problem. The woman at the door took note of our southern accents and looked us over suspiciously. 'No,' she said, 'I can't help you, but there's some of your kind living down the road – the house beside the bridge on this side.' Our kind? Catholics? We didn't call to the house beside the bridge but wheeled our bikes on and out of sight as we tried to decide what to do. This was a strange place, and we were glad we were only spending a couple of days in it.

Shortly afterwards, an ice-cream van pulled up, and the two young men inside offered to bring us and our bikes to the next town. They were friendly and asked lots of questions. On hearing we were from the Republic, they declared that they were Unionists. This seemed quaint, like Royalist or Puritan, and didn't mean much to us, but within a year we would all know what Unionist, Loyalist, Nationalist and Republican stood for as the Troubles erupted across the North.

The following summer, after our Leaving Cert, we hitchhiked around the highlands of Scotland, drawn by the romance of the Jacobite rebellion. But it was a bit of a let-down as the landscapes were like those at home, only much wetter and full of midges. This was to be Bairbre's last month of freedom. In the autumn she left for the novitiate of the Faithful Companions of Jesus in Broadstairs, Kent, and I started studying in University College Dublin. This was the first time that our lives had diverged, but it wasn't for long: Bairbre came home after three months, having decided that the religious life was not for her after all.

I didn't know any of the other 10,000 students in UCD, and,

being just a recent seventeen, I found the social side of college life a bit overwhelming. This wasn't surprising as I still hadn't made the acquaintance of a single boy.

I had chosen English as one of my subjects, and on the very first day there was a minor controversy because *Lolita* was included on our reading list. A small group of nuns had left a note on the lecturer's desk asking that they be excused from reading the scandalous novel. They were embarking on degree courses so that they could teach in convent secondary schools – schools that were suddenly expanding as free secondary education had just come in. Nuns had the privilege of their own private reading room, and even their own separate toilets, in the dark overcrowded university building in Earlsfort Terrace. But this was 1969, and the lecturer was scathing in his refusal to grant their request. My own knowledge and experience of sex was so limited that I could have done with an exemption myself as I got to grips with Humbert Humbert.

Philosophy was my other main subject, and the existentialists were all the rage. There were over 1,000 doing first-year philosophy, and they all had brand-new copies of Sartre's *Existentialism and Humanism*, a little red hardcover with a white dust jacket. My book had a dull grey cover and had long lost its jacket. It was a first edition of the English translation and had come from my aunt who was the county librarian in Cavan. She had passed it on to my parents when some of Sartre's works were banned by the Censorship of Publications Board a decade earlier.

Were Sartre's books not banned anymore? It seemed that all the old certainties were being overturned in 1969. One way or the other, I felt that my possession of such a seasoned-looking copy could only add to my image as an intellectual, as I sat alone through every lecture.

'Well, *I* don't believe in God,' said the girl walking out of the philosophy tutorial with me. She spoke very casually, as if this was something you could just say. This wasn't Mia Farrow in *Peyton Place* or some San Francisco flower child, this was a very ordinary girl from the north side of Dublin. And she didn't believe in God? My mind changed gear, and I was soon as convinced of Sartre's views on the meaning of life as I had been of Sister Winifred's. Yes, of course life was absurd. I agreed with Marx too, about religion being the opium of the people. It was all so obvious now. All those stories and rules and threats of eternal damnation and that reassuring explanation for existence – none of it was credible anymore.

Bairbre and I were still living at home, and I put three posters up on the wall on my side of our room. Two of them were black and white: Karl Marx, looking elderly and wise, and James Joyce as a young man, lounging, hands in pockets, in front of a glasshouse. The third poster was of Che Guevara – the new red and black one that made him look like Jesus. In the space of a year I had gone from yearning to enter a convent to being a convinced atheist with a scorn for all religious belief.

Second Year began with a philosophy conference entitled 'The Meaning of Meaning', but that was the last time I gave meaning much thought as life suddenly became a lot more interesting. Bairbre was studying Arts now too, and we crossed paths as we wandered the brand-new concrete Arts Block in Belfield. The big concourses smelled of rubber and were strange inhospitable places until the clubs and societies set out their wares for Freshers' Week. Then we discovered the mountaineering club. The new members' stand was festooned with boots, helmets and ropes, and there was a display of books and posters showing mountains and cliffs and ice and snow. This was the place for us!

'Bairbre, you're not going out dressed like that!' said my father sharply as we lifted our rucksacks to head out one Sunday morning a few months later. Bairbre was wearing her pride and joy: a pair of tan-coloured corduroy knee breeches. She had bought them second-hand from Jimmy Murphy, the captain/secretary of the mountaineering club, for five pounds, and she wore a pair of thick red woollen knee socks pulled up to them. The breeches were the real thing, but they were designed for hefty bearded alpinists not nineteen-year-old girls. They would be a bit eye-catching out at the

Loughlinstown bus stop on the Bray Road.

'I certainly am!' she retorted, and we left, anxious not to miss the club bus from town.

'We'll get Mass along the way,' I said vaguely, but no one was really asking. I usually skipped Mass whenever I could without it being too obvious to my parents, but Bairbre continued to attend regularly. Times were changing though, and it didn't seem to be such a definite mortal sin anymore, even to her, to miss Sunday Mass.

The UCD Mountaineering Club organised hill walks in the Wicklow Mountains every Sunday, and we found ourselves, for the first time ever, in the easy company of like-minded young people. Soon we'd had lunch on the top of every boggy mountain in Wicklow and had forged strong friendships with about a dozen lads and girls who loved being out in the hills as much as we did. Those friendships were to shape all our years in college.

At the end of a day's walk we'd cover long heel-blistering miles on little tarred roads to the pub. We wouldn't turn on our head torches, even when it was fully dark, as that would waste the batteries and ruin everyone's night vision. Walking along in the dark with a lad you might fancy had a special intimacy, in spite of the ring of a dozen pairs of boots on the road up ahead.

The pubs we ended up in – Tutty's of Hollywood, Fenton's in the Glen of Imaal or Healy's of Roundwood – were warm friendly places where the barmen never objected to us taking out the last of our sandwiches to go with the crisps and Guinness. One wet evening we were in Tutty's when Jimmy, our much-admired captain, moved close to the open fire to dry his damp trousers.

'Here, young fella,' said an old man who was sitting there. 'Ye're all students, are ye?'

'Yeah,' said Jimmy.

'And tell me this: what are them young ones like for sex? Are they good, bein' students an' all?' Jimmy reddened and glared at him. 'Or do ye only go for the good-lookin' ones? If ye ask me they're one as good as another – shur ye don't be lookin' at the mantelpiece when ye'r pokin' the fire!'

Jimmy scowled and turned away. Ours was an innocent and inexperienced group, and those of us who'd heard the old fellow were very embarrassed. He left the pub soon after, and if he hadn't we would have.

On St Stephen's Day in 1970 we headed south on a week-long club trip to Kerry. The Climber's Inn, Jack Walsh's well-known pub-cum-hostel, was at the foot of the MacGillycuddy Reeks. One morning, Bairbre and I set out to do the Reeks Walk, the long demanding traverse that takes in most of the highest summits in the range. It looked quite feasible on the half-inch map. We weren't particularly fit, and the initial haul up Caher from Lough Acoose was hard going, but then the further rise to the top of Carrauntoohil went easily enough. We could retrace our steps from the summit – that would be a good day's walk in itself, especially in midwinter – or we could go on. As we were at the highest point in Ireland, the rest of the walk was going to be sort of downhill. We were feeling fine and we decided to go on.

The weather deteriorated when we got to the big saddle above the Devil's Ladder gully. We identified the gully on the map but knew there was no point in descending there as we'd be miles from the Gap of Dunloe where we had arranged to be picked up. We tackled the next wide grassy slope at a reasonable pace, but then the sky lowered and the mist rolled in. Still, we were making good time along the broad ridge and were able to follow the rising ground without having to constantly check our compass bearing. We reckoned we must be three-quarters of the way along our walk by now.

Soon the short turf gave way to rocky ground, and fingers of jagged ridge loomed out of the murk. We'd reached Cummenapeasta, the narrow crest that edged the steep drop down to the 'coum of the *péist* (monster)' on the north side. The coum, or corrie, was a big bite out of the hillside, and it cupped the small lake that was reputed to be home to the *péist*. We had our own worrying myths about the ridge. Some said it was grand and just needed a bit of care; others said it was fierce and that you had to make a fingertip traverse above an abyss. By now our woollen balaclavas and gloves were soaked and the wet was seeping through our cagoules.

The light began to fade and with it the last of our optimism. We had head torches but knew better than to tackle dangerous terrain on a winter's night. We'd been on steep rocky ground before, ground where one misstep onto a shaky block would send an electric shock of warning across your pelvic floor – an intimate reminder that a moment's inattention could be fatal. And even if we did make it across the sharp ridge, would our map and compass skills get us the rest of the way to the Gap of Dunloe in the dark? We agreed to head down off the exposed ridge, straight down the steep south side to the Black Valley.

The beams of our head torches illuminated just a few metres of ground at a time, and the dips and rises of the slope confused us until we weren't sure if we were going downhill or wandering sideways. We hit a stream and followed its steep rush as best we could until we saw a light approach from below. It was a farmer with a torch: he had spotted our erratic pinpoints of light in the blackness and had come to guide us down. We were very grateful and even more so when he said he'd drive us around to the Gap of Dunloe if we paid for the petrol.

Much later, warm and dry in the bar in Jack Walsh's, we spun all the hours of tension and harsh effort, all the falls and slides, the hidden pools and treacherous little cliffs, into an epic tale for the rest of our group. It was intoxicating stuff.

Halfway through the week, four hill walkers, all male, arrived down from Dublin. 'Spillikin Club,' said Jimmy quietly as they strolled into the bar. These must be real climbers, real mountaineers, if they were members of the legendary Spillikin Club. When they checked the dorms for space and realised how strictly we had segregated ourselves into boys' rooms and girls' rooms, they were amused. 'At least we sleep with our women,' commented one of them. So these fellows had women? And they slept with them? This was all a bit disconcerting. Were they married? How could they speak so casually and shamelessly about sex? They were obviously different from us, and a bit dangerous. And where were their women anyway? But we didn't concern ourselves with them and soon dismissed their scorn. We were in no rush to break out of the safe boundaries of our conservative middle-class social scene.

The following Easter there was a club trip to Connemara. It's said that the sun dances on Easter Sunday morning, and it woke me as it lit up our tents on the hill above Killary Harbour. When we'd arrived the previous night it had been a struggle to pitch the tents in a strong wind, but now the air was calm and beginning to warm up. I unzipped the door and found the great grey-green mass of Mweelrea mountain filling the view. Its ridged flanks rose straight out of the narrow fjord, and if you had the seven-league boots of fairytales you could step across the water and stride right up it. Over the following few days we strode up onto the fine rocky summits of the Twelve Bens and the Maumturks and stood with our friends looking out over the twisted Connemara coastline. And that had a magic all its own.

Our first year in the UCD Mountaineering Club, 1970/1971, was also the year when adventure sports first became visible in Ireland. Activities like climbing and canoeing were already well developed in Britain, having grown out of the strong British tradition of outdoor recreation. There was a view across the water, a Protestant view, that engaging in wholesome physical pursuits was an admirable form of Christian manliness. Added to that, the risk-taking element of adventure activities had long been legitimised, for men at least, by the exploits of heroes such as Robert Falcon Scott and Sir Edmund Hillary.

The ground was not as fertile in Ireland when it came to such ventures. Bairbre was managing the mountaineering club stand for college Freshers' Week in 1972 when a priest came by and started giving out to her for putting her God-given body at risk through mountaineering. She was startled into silence and only came up with her killer reply after the man had left: 'What about that pope, Pope Pius XI? He climbed Mont Blanc *and* the Matterhorn!' But she and I had moved well beyond the reach of clerics by then. Far from seeing our bodies as a moral liability, we were now part of a brave new world of mountaineers, canoeists, cavers, surfers and orienteers. And there was not a single Laurel Hill-style young lady in sight.

Established mountaineers Joss Lynam and Paddy O'Leary had set up the Association for Adventure Sports (AFAS) in 1969 and were soon organising courses in all sorts of exciting activities. Along with our friend Sheila Willis, Bairbre and I signed up for the mountain-leadership course. Being a mountain leader meant that you were qualified to bring groups hill walking in Ireland, but we were doing it mainly as a way of becoming competent mountaineers.

There was already one Irish female mountain leader – Trina Cleary – who had trained in Scotland, and we listened with interest to her tales of a summer trip to the Austrian Alps where she'd had to use a plastic pipe to suck water up from between boulders, there being no other water available, and had cut the handle off her toothbrush to reduce the weight she carried in her rucksack.

For the leadership-training weekends, the three of us went to the mountains of Kerry and Connemara and to the newly opened National Adventure Centre in Tiglin, County Wicklow. Sometimes just one of us would be free to go on a scheduled weekend, sometimes two, but whatever the permutation, Bairbre and I knew that we were lucky to have Sheila as a friend. She shared our values and ambitions and, most importantly, got on very well with each of us even when we got annoyed with each other.

In Tiglin, where Paddy O'Leary was the director, we picked up camping skills and learned how to light brass Primus stoves using methylated spirits and paraffin – the stoves hadn't changed since the days of Scott of the Antarctic. And we learned enough first aid to be able to tie triangular bandages and hope that we never came across a casualty with a haemopneumothorax. We also learned that single most essential skill for the independent mountaineer: how to navigate on wild pathless uplands. At that time, in the early 1970s, Croagh Patrick was the only mountain in Ireland that had a path up it, and there were so few regular hill walkers that if you spotted someone in Dublin with a proper rucksack you expected to recognise them.

We found that mastering the use of a compass was only half the navigation story as it took a lot of experience and cunning to interpret the secrets of the half-inch Ordnance Survey maps. A finger-width of map, with its mustard-coloured shading to denote high ground, could look innocuous on paper while the actual terrain might turn out to be an obstacle course of boulders, small crags, scree slopes and bogholes. We did solo walks and discovered how the land lays more claim to you when you're completely alone. You settle to your pace, undistracted, and your thoughts lose their thickness as you notice the smell of the heather and the bog pools that mirror the ever-changing light.

We slept out in the mountains without a tent, cosy in our sleeping bags beneath the stars, and called it a bivy (the mountaineers' term for a bivouac). And we prepared for the big weekend, the winter-skills course, by kitting ourselves out with borrowed ice axes and crampons – the most exciting bits of equipment that a hill walker is ever likely to use. We camped high on the flank of Carrauntoohil that weekend, with a dozen others, and hoped for snow. The instructors included a few volunteers from the Spillikin Club, and Sheila and I were keen to impress them by showing that we were ready for anything the mountains might throw at us. But the weather was of the drizzly heads-down hoods-up kind, and no icy gullies or snow-cloaked buttresses appeared out of the mist to let us demonstrate our growing confidence as mountaineers.

For our night walk (another training requirement), Sheila and I were glad that it was going to be just the two of us and we'd be free to make all our own decisions. We chose to go to Glendalough, the scenic valley in the heart of the Wicklow Mountains. As with Gougane Barra in West Cork, the combination of lake, forest and rocky hillside had made the valley an enticing retreat for early Christian monks and hermits. For us its main attraction was that we could get there by public transport. We reckoned that the big ring of Glendalough would be a good undertaking. It was a long circuit, and in the boggy central section, high above the back end of the valley, there was an elusive lake that we would take in in passing. Hill walkers often stumbled on Lough Firrib by accident, or missed it altogether, and we knew that our skill in navigating to it in the dark would look impressive in our logbooks.

We planned the route carefully and calculated all our distances, times and compass bearings in advance. It was reassuring to have those precise figures noted down on a piece of paper, though we knew how easy it was to stray from a compass bearing in mist or darkness, or to get completely confused when a looming peat hag – a little cliff of bog – suggested a rearing mountain summit where we knew there shouldn't be one.

We got the St Kevin's bus to the village of Laragh in the evening and set off to walk the last 4 kilometres to where the road ended in the depths of the Glendalough valley. There, by the big Upper Lake, would be our starting point. It was already dark when we got off the bus, and it was only when we passed the last of the street lights at the Royal Hotel that we realised how pitch black it was. We couldn't make out the famous round tower in the field just to the left of the road. We couldn't even see the road. It hadn't crossed our minds to wait for a moonlit night.

We were saving our head-torch batteries and tried to keep to the middle of the tarred surface of the road, guided by the faint outline of black treetops against the dark sky. As we got close to the car park we were beginning to reconsider. Maybe we should just settle for the small ring, the much shorter circuit via Derrybawn Mountain? Just then, Sheila walked straight into a concrete post and nearly knocked herself out. We gave up. We pitched our tent in the trees just beyond the car park, out of sight of any early-morning ramblers, and got the bus home the next day.

We gradually ticked off the requirements for the course and got a lot of experience leading walks for our college club, but as Sheila and I were preparing for our final exams we deferred our assessment until the following year. This left the way clear for Bairbre to become the first Irish-trained female mountain leader – an achievement all three of us were quietly proud of.

AFAS was the body providing the training, assessment and certification for the leadership course, with the details being worked out, mainly, by Joss Lynam. Joss was everywhere. He was a mountaineer and an orienteer, and, as someone with a passionate interest in promoting adventure sports, he was in his element in this new era of training and qualifications. He was a tireless organiser and committee member, and when Bairbre, and later Sheila and I, were presented with our mountain-leadership certificates, they were signed by him on behalf of the Federation of Mountaineering Clubs of Ireland (FMCI). The FMCI was the new national body for the still idiosyncratic activity of mountaineering that my father had introduced us to in the Caha Mountains in 1961.

Chapter 4

'Girls don't climb,' said a senior (female) member of the mountaineering club to Sheila when we talked of starting to rock climb in the spring of 1971. She meant that though hill walking was an acceptable activity for girls, climbing – actually pulling yourself up steep rock by your own strength – certainly wasn't. *Huh*, we thought, *if the boys are climbing and it's fun, then we're going to climb too.*

Of course we were going to climb. It was the gateway to real mountaineering, and it sounded not just fun but wildly exciting. It would be a whole new way of using our bodies – bodies that we still knew little about – and it even had its own vocabulary. When your arms got really tired, you were 'pumped', or you might get 'sewing-machine leg' when nervous tension made your leg jig up and down uncontrollably on a small foothold. We heard too that if you were able to lead climbs that were hard enough to be labelled 'Very Severe', then you really were somebody.

Jimmy, our club captain, had dark curly hair and dancing eyes and was fun to be with. We hung on his every word. When he first brought five of us girls, and some of the boys, climbing in Dalkey Quarry that spring, we had no idea what to expect. We'd never seen anyone climb, not even on television, and the pictures in books were often confusing, especially about what part the rope played in it all.

We gathered in Dalkey Quarry at the southern end of Dublin Bay every Saturday and were soon using exotic words like 'karabiner' and 'belay' and 'abseil'. Jimmy showed us how to tie the rope around our waists and secure it with a bowline knot (climbing harnesses only became available the following year) and how to fasten our borrowed helmets. We learned to shout 'Climbing!' in response to his 'Climb when ready', and then, as he took in the rope from above, one of us would set off, pulling on knobs and edges and scanning the steep slabs for bumps to step on in this new world of rising rock.

Dalkey Quarry's pale walls were a natural theatre where we could watch each other climb, oblivious to the passing dog-walkers. We wore old corduroy jeans and fraying jumpers and borrowed climbing shoes. You could wear runners, or walking boots, but the neat climbing shoes with their smooth rubber soles seemed to work wonders, especially for us girls who depended much more on our footwork than on our arm strength.

We pored over the gear catalogues from the Ellis Brigham climbing shops, which were works of art – but the nearest shop was in North Wales. Eventually Bairbre and I took the train to Belfast to buy our own rock shoes in Jackson's sports shop in Bedford Street. It was the only place on the whole island that sold shoes for rock climbing. Mr Jackson, the owner, was impressed that we'd make the journey, given the times that were in it, and we were brought out the back for tea and currant buns.

This was in 1972, and the Troubles were rising to their murderous height. The shop was bombed out five years later while the violence still raged. No one was hurt, but the building was destroyed in the subsequent fire. In due course, Jackson's reopened in a different premises a few streets away. The shop had been bombed because it was a Protestant business – it was nothing personal.

Belaying is an essential skill for climbing, and we learned it early on. The standard climbing unit is two people with a rope: while one climbs, the other protects them by managing the rope and anchoring it to prevent a fall turning into a catastrophe. Belaying works upwards and downwards. As the leader climbs and clips the rope to gear slotted into cracks, the belayer feeds the rope out from below, ready to hang onto it in case of a fall, and then when the leader is well anchored at the top, they draw the rope up as the second follows. In both cases, the rope is pulled through a friction device on the belayer's harness, where it jams if it is subject to the sudden jerk of a fall. You use the same friction device when you're abseiling by letting your rope slide slowly through it as you walk backwards down the rock face.

As soon as Bairbre and Sheila and I, and our two female friends, had learned to belay each other, we were able to come to Dalkey to climb independently whenever a couple of us were free. Public transport was poor, but we had all bought little red Honda 50 motorbikes, second-hand, and were able to save ourselves a lot of time waiting on buses that didn't come. We weren't intent on a girls-only endeavour, but for a while we were the keenest climbers in our college group. Climbing permeated our lives, and we felt we were living more intensely than the rest of humankind who'd never had the chance to step onto rock.

It was during our second climbing season, in 1972, that Bairbre and Sheila and I started to lead climbs. When you were seconding and finding the going tough, you could shout 'Tight rope', and your leader would haul in any slack on the rope until there was a bit of an upward pull. This was very reassuring: it might even be enough to help you through the hard bit, and it meant that if you did fall you weren't going to go far. But when you were leading, the rope was below you, shocking in its uselessness as it hung slackly from your harness. If you fell you'd drop.

Of course you could minimise the drop. We learned how to jam the aluminium protection wedges into cracks and clip our ropes to them as we climbed so that if we fell, we would end up dangling underneath the protection while our second held the rope tight from below. The gear you clipped to should stop you hitting the ground in the event of a fall, but you always went further than you expected because the rope was designed to stretch – to absorb the shock and minimise the jolt on your body. You would usually hang in your climbing harness unscathed after a fall, unless of course your protection pulled out and you fell to the ground. You could never predict the outcome of a fall, and the golden rule was 'The leader never falls.' The clear message was that you should never attempt to lead a climb unless you were fairly sure that you were able to get up it.

How would you know that if you'd never been on the climb before? This was where the guidebook came in. Climbing guidebooks had brief informative notes on each climb. These notes followed a formula that included a historical record – who had climbed it first and when – as well as some technical details such as the exact location of the climb, the height of it, a description of where to go on the rock (e.g., climb the crack, ramp, groove or wall, etc.) and the grade of difficulty one might expect.

The grade was the most crucial of these, and we girls often disagreed vehemently with the grade given in the guidebook for a particular climb. All of the climbs were graded by men and for men, as there were very few women climbing, and the grades corresponded with what men thought to be easy or hard. We found that moves requiring the sort of brute strength that we didn't have were often undergraded while delicate manoeuvres involving good balance and footwork were, for us, less demanding for their given grade.

We had a dread of running out of strength on a strenuous move, maybe an attempt to pull up a steep section of rock with just one good handhold – the sort of move that wouldn't cost the lads a thought – and hanging there with all the weight on one arm, unable to go up or down until your fingers uncurled and you fell off. When I gathered my wits after falling off a climb in Dalkey, I heard someone screaming and realised it was me. I hadn't fallen far, but I'd had no gear in and had landed on my coccyx on a pointy rock. The pain was excruciating, but it turned out that I hadn't done any lasting damage.

Dalkey Quarry was an easy place to hurt yourself. There weren't many cracks or slots in the quarried granite where you could put gear in, and if you did fall when leading there seemed to be lots of ledges and bulges to hit before the rope came tight. We didn't dare take the guidebook grades at face value, and when we started leading we were very cautious, choosing climbs at the lowest grades of difficulty that we already knew from seconding (following someone else up them while having the security of a rope from above).

The grading system began with Moderate – the sort of easy scrambling that we had done as children – and progressed through a series of awkward adjectives: Difficult, Very Difficult, Severe, Hard Severe, Very Severe, Hard Very Severe and Extremely Severe. Some of these were known by abbreviations: V Diff, VS, HVS and XS. We couldn't imagine what an XS might be like – it was beyond the reach of all but a handful of the top Irish climbers at the time. For us, leading Hard Severe was a breakthrough. It was the fifth one up, and climbs given that grade always seemed to be awkward and strenuous.

Leading took nerve, and I always felt a tightening in my insides when I tied onto the 'sharp' end of the rope. We rarely fell, and usually didn't hurt ourselves when we did, but Sheila broke her leg in a leader fall and Bairbre had a 'ground' fall too, but we three found that leading climbs was by far the most exhilarating thing we had ever done. We never considered top-roping to quicken our progress. This was when you organised to have the security of a rope from above before you attempted a climb. This was seen as a form of cheating and was unacceptable in the mountaineering ethos of the time.

In the quarry we crossed paths with the wider climbing community, particularly on Thursday nights when everyone ended up in McDonagh's pub in Dalkey village. It was always crowded, and we'd squeeze through to the bar past climbers we'd heard about and looked up to, such as Paul McHugh, Sé Billane and Emmett Goulding, who were all members of the Spillikin Club. Only the best climbers could join the Spillikin Club as you had to have led some hard routes before you could apply for membership.

In the pub we'd hear the Spillikin climbers talk about the Alps, about what so-and-so had done there the previous summer and about the plans anyone had for the coming season. It was always the French Alps they spoke of, and Chamonix, the mountain town where everyone stayed, echoed again and again through their conversation. Chamonix was the epicentre of hard climbing in the early 1970s. The Alps are full of mountains that you can walk up, like Mont Blanc, but serious alpinists are drawn to the challenge of long, steep, technically demanding climbs, on rock and ice, and Chamonix was recognised as having the greatest concentration of these in the world. Now that we were leading climbs, Bairbre and Sheila and I felt that we were entering the exciting realm of glorious mountaineering exploits, and Chamonix was the byword for all our alpine dreams.

Another Thursday night regular was Joss Lynam. He was the embodiment of the senior mountaineer with his greying beard and encyclopaedic knowledge of all things mountaineering. It felt good to be able to wish him luck for his upcoming Irish Greenland Expedition. Expeditions were the ultimate adventure.

There were very few women among the climbers in Dalkey, and we never saw any of them leading. There had been a handful of independent women climbers in Ireland during the 1950s and 1960s, but none of them seemed to be active anymore. There was one name that we kept hearing: that of Betty Healy. Betty was a member of the Irish Mountaineering Club, and she had not only led climbs at a high standard but had done some first ascents in Glendalough and on high mountain crags in Donegal. We were impressed to hear this, but Betty had stopped climbing by the early 1970s, and we never ran into her in the quarry. Our motivation was each other and the books we read about climbs in the Alps and the Himalayas, and that's where we hoped we'd be headed too, once we got the hang of this rock climbing.

Nobody trained for climbing or if they did they kept it secret. Natural talent and courage were what made a good climber, and time spent on press-ups or lifting weights was seen as a bit suspect. We were sitting with our club friends in the sun in Dalkey one day when I wondered aloud if we girls would develop bulging muscles from all this climbing. Barry, a postgrad science student, said that we needn't worry, that our jeans wouldn't allow it. I shifted a bit uncomfortably. Were our jeans that tight?

'No, you needn't worry,' he went on. 'Your female genes definitely won't allow it.' Oh . . . right. Of course, he was a scientist and he'd know about that sort of thing. We certainly didn't. At school we'd played hockey, netball and tennis, but we just went out and played, for better or worse, without any awareness of our muscles or how they might be trained.

In the early 1970s, the words 'woman', 'fitness' and 'strength' were simply never heard in the same sentence. When Bairbre and Sheila and I made our first tentative moves up steep rock in 1971, no woman had yet got to the top of Everest, and women were not permitted to run in marathons. When it came to strenuous exercise, there were dire warnings about the possible effects on the female body. My aunt, the librarian, warned me about the damage climbing might do to my reproductive system. She herself was thankful that she had a career – rare enough for an Irish woman of her generation – and had escaped the hard life on the family farm where strong muscles were the result of drudgery.

Then there was all the repression that went with the young-lady ideal. The Victorian-era saying, 'Horses sweat and men perspire but ladies only glow' still held currency, and many people thought that refinement, particularly physical refinement, was an essential aspect of femininity. In our convent boarding school we had been taught that self-control trumped all other virtues and that strict management of the body, while unmentionable, was the cornerstone of an acceptable life. We controlled our teenage bodies with corsets, or roll-ons as we called them (the suspenders on them kept our nylon stockings up until tights appeared towards the end of the 1960s). As we grew to womanhood it was a case of strap it up and wrap it up and don't expect much from it. Strengthening muscles and investigating the body's possibilities was certainly not something a nice girl would do.

That summer, Bairbre and I went climbing in the Pyrenees. We set our sights on the highest mountain in Andorra. It was Bairbre's idea of course. The Pyrenees had a mild reputation compared to the Alps, but the draw of this peak, the Coma Pedrosa, was that it sat at the junction of three frontiers – of Andorra, France and Spain – and its summit height was over 3,000 metres. There was no actual climbing involved – you're only climbing if you have to use your hands – but it was exotic enough and distant enough to scare us and excite us in equal measure.

It took us three days to get to the top and back down again, and we spent a lot of that time avoiding men. This was our first trip abroad, and after getting a one-way student flight to Barcelona, we'd stayed for a week at the Mediterranean coast but were unnerved by the amount of attention we drew as two unaccompanied girls. Wherever we went men and boys would follow us and make comments and try to engage us in conversation. Some of them said we must be Swedish. Swedish? Yes, Swedish girls walk around on their own and believe in free love. Oh no, we assured them, in our best school Spanish, we're from little Catholic Ireland, and it's not like that over there. Then we quickly packed away our swimming togs and started hitching to Andorra.

Once we got to the foothills of the Pyrenees it was hard to find somewhere cheap to stay. We were advised to go up to La Molina, a winter ski resort, where there would probably be rooms available. There weren't many cars going that way, but one pulled up, and the driver, a young man, wound down the window to ask me where we were headed. He said the ski resort wasn't on his route but that he'd drop us up there as a favour, in return for a kiss. I laughed and agreed, and in we got.

I regretted the deal immediately, and the closer we came to La Molina the more uneasy I became. What if he wasn't joking? I felt like Bluebeard's wife, out on her balcony watching for her husband's return and dreading the moment of reckoning. When we got to the village, Bairbre went into the hotel to make enquiries. She just shrugged when I asked her what I should do. Alone in the car I let the driver kiss me – I felt obliged to keep my side of the bargain. But I hadn't expected a kiss like that. It was a serious kiss, and it was a revelation. How could a stranger make you feel . . . like that? I thought you had to be in love with someone before you'd feel that you were melting inside. I thought it was all about what went on inside your head, or mostly anyway, but here was the body taking over. So that was what the nuns had been on about! That was why management of the body was such a big deal!

The young man asked me if I'd ever been kissed like that before, and when I said I hadn't, he was incredulous. 'You're eighteen and you've never been kissed like that?' I felt naive and childish – and it was worse than that: I was almost nineteen and had already finished two years in college. And I was afraid of what might happen next. Bairbre came back just then to say that even the cheapest room in the hotel was quite expensive, too expensive for our budget. I said we'd take it anyway, and we thanked the driver for the lift.

Politeness had kept me in the car. When I was fifteen, one night I was being driven home by a man whose children I'd been babysitting. He put an exploratory hand on my thigh as he drove. I pushed it away, and neither of us said anything. What did he want with me? I knew he had a pretty wife. I was embarrassed, doubly embarrassed. Had I misread the situation? Was he offended? When he pulled up outside my parents' house, I made a half apology. (*I* apologised to *him*?) Little did the nuns know but politeness and refinement could be the death of you.

On our way up the Coma Pedrosa we came across some little huts that were designated as mountain refuges. They were all empty, but we were afraid to go near them in daylight in case we were spotted. There was the shepherd to worry about and the couple of walkers we'd passed, and we were especially wary of a cheery group of hunters who'd come over a rocky crest from France just as it started to get dark. Were they really hunters? Wasn't that a very theatrical-looking rabbit the first one had hanging from his belt?

We settled into one of the huts but were afraid that our flickering candle might betray us. In the morning our courage came back with the sun, but the second night was no better. We were above all the huts now and had to bivouac in a shallow cave. We'd been warned that there might be bandits in the mountains, and even bears, and with some misgivings we lit a fire and took turns keeping watch beside it.

When we eventually made it to the top of the mountain we were very pleased with ourselves and took hazy photographs of the dry grey peaks and ridges that ran off into France and Spain.

And now it was time to head home. We got the usual mix of lifts – good ones to hostels and bad ones to motorway junctions where it was illegal to stand with your thumb out. It was mostly truck drivers who picked us up, and time and again the Spanish truckers tut-tutted at the risks we were taking and wanted to bring us home to stay with their families. We didn't see it that way: every youth hostel in France was full of young people flicking confidently through the *International Hostellers' Handbook*, and everybody hitchhiked.

But here in Franco's Spain things were different. There weren't many hitchhikers, and the police were armed, but worst of all a lot of the hostels were either closed or being used for children's summer camps. One evening we ended up at a convent. '*Quièn llama*?' demanded a voice from a third-floor window. This was so embarrassing. When we'd found the local hostel all locked up, our truck driver had insisted on bringing us here, to a convent, to an orphanage! A nun had come out onto a high balcony, and after the driver had explained his mission, she came down and let us in.

The orphanage was empty for the summer, and we slept on little iron beds with our feet sticking out at the end. In the morning, the nun served us coffee, hard bread and chorizo. We'd never seen salami before. The raw-looking orangey meat with its pimples of fat and chewy oily gristle revolted us, and we had to stick the half-eaten pieces up our sleeves.

When we crossed the border and made our way up through France, we noticed that most of the big trucks had beds behind the front seat. We got used to the drivers mentioning them and making suggestions, half joking, half chancing their luck. We felt safe enough since there were two of us. But then one driver pulled into a lay-by and wouldn't take no for an answer. I was sitting in the middle, and he grabbed me and held a knife to my throat. Our French was good enough to understand his threats, but luckily for me I couldn't see the knife – I thought it was his ring that was sticking into me.

Bairbre stayed cool too. 'Stop that ridiculous nonsense!' she said in her most withering Mother Dympna tone, and then she said it again, in French. And he did. He cursed us and threw us out, and the truck took off at speed. Our rucksacks were gone, with our money and our boots and the presents for everyone at home – a disaster!

We hesitated, not knowing whether to run after the truck or into the bushes, but just then it grated to a halt in a spray of gravel. We froze as the door opened, but the driver didn't appear. He flung our rucksacks out onto the ground and roared away.

We were both shocked, but we didn't discuss it. There really wasn't anything to say, and as we didn't have the money for buses or trains, we'd have to carry on hitching anyway. We weren't deeply upset by our close escape as we had no real understanding of sexual violence. When it came to matters of sex we were adrift on a sea of ignorance, bobbing uneasily between the old prohibitions of the Catholic Church and the startling new liberties of the sexual revolution. We thought that while rape must be much worse than having your wallet stolen, it was somewhere on the same scale. You'd get over it, unless of course you got pregnant, and then there really would be trouble. We were back at the side of the road a few minutes later, with our thumbs out and hopeful looks on our faces.

When we got home, we regaled our parents with selected tales of our Pyrenean adventures and told our club friends about all the rest. We settled back to another happy year of college life, but by the following spring I was beginning to draw away from the club as I moved onto harder climbs and into the company of more elite climbers. My first breakthrough was in Glendalough, on the big cliff that lies towards the back of the valley, beyond the end of the lake.

I had first climbed on that crag during a club trip the previous year. It hadn't looked very impressive when we'd stopped to view it from the approach track. It was just a sunlit rise of rock on a heathery hillside. But by the time we got to the foot of it we could see how its great granite buttresses reared up to three times the height of Dalkey Quarry.

Jimmy had eight or nine of us in tow that day, all novice climbers who listened eagerly to his tales of the 'epics' that seasoned climbers had had on the grooves and cracks in the walls above us. He knew what all the foreign words in the climbing terminology meant, words that had been borrowed from French alpinism. An 'arête' was a narrow ridge, and 'couloirs' and 'cols' were gullies and saddles, and though he hadn't been climbing very long himself, Jimmy had excellent climbing credentials – he had led *Very Severe* climbs. VS was the grade of difficulty above Hard Severe, and it marked a new level of engagement with the rock. Most reasonably fit able-bodied people could shuffle up a climb graded Diff, V Diff, Severe or even Hard Severe, if they had enough encouragement and a tight rope from above, but when you got to Very Severe it took skill and flair to solve the riddle of the rock.

'And look up there,' said Jimmy, his hand sweeping up towards the highest point of the cliff. 'That's Spillikin – Spillikin Ridge.' Yes, we'd heard of that one. It was probably the best-known climb in the country, and the pegs on it had held a lot of falls. I wondered what it would be like to climb high above the ground on rock so steep that even the best climbers – all men of course – had to use 'aid' to get up the crux (the hardest section).

Jimmy explained that you used aid when your fingers grasping the rock just weren't enough and you had to pull on equipment to move up through the crux. The equipment was steel pegs hammered into cracks, and once a peg was securely in place, and the climber had clipped their rope to it, it could be used as a handhold, a foothold or even an anchor point for a dangling rest. Using aid was a last resort for getting past a crux section, and if another climber repeated the climb 'free' – without the peg – they were climbing in a better style than you.

In the early 1970s, Spillikin Ridge was one of the hardest climbs in Ireland, and the day I went to lead my first Very Severe in 1973, I found myself right up there beside its scary bulges. My climb, which was called Nightmare, followed easier-angled rock just to the left, but Spillikin's aura added to the sense of exposure.

Exposure – the feeling of being way up there with little security and a lot of space beneath your feet – didn't usually bother me. I always liked being high up on a cliff and well clear of the ground in case of a fall, but now the swell of rock beside me emphasised the drop below. Was that where I'd swing if I fell or would I land back down on my second? I was with a friend from Tiglin, and it was just the two of us on a little ledge halfway up the crag.

The Glendalough cliff was too high to be climbed in one go so you had to do it in two or three rope lengths or pitches. The leader (who was almost always male apart from me) would climb up to a ledge and belay or anchor himself there and then take in the spare rope to secure his partner as he or she climbed in turn. Who led what pitch depended on the capability and nerve of each of the pair. Some people, particularly girlfriends, never led. And people who never led were not real climbers. They never felt the electrifying excitement that risk brings, nor the surge of power that comes from controlling your fear and breaking through the limitations of the voice in your head.

On the lower part of the cliff, I'd waltzed up Prelude, a nice easy climb where you could move lightly up and away from the clutches of gravity, but now we were on the small ledge below the steep crux wall of Nightmare. I knew from seconding it that I'd find it hard. My partner adjusted his anchor attachments and sat back, ready to pay out the rope. He could relax a little, but I was full of nervous energy. I checked the knot on my harness and the small selection of gear I had hanging from it. The rock above had no crack wide enough for me to jam in a piece of protection, but there was a rusty peg sticking out of a thin seam.

I tugged at it, and it felt solid. It should stop me falling too far. I clipped my rope to it and ran my fingers up and down a vertical edge, searching for the best roughnesses for my fingertips. I latched onto the edge, one hand above the other, then stepped up on a small wrinkle and pulled hard. My arms took most of my weight as I moved up, and they immediately signalled panic. I grabbed the vertical edge higher up with my right hand and snatched a small hold with the left before stepping up again. Now the rock was pushing me out as I hung there, one foot scrabbling for something to stand on, the other wavering on a little nick. My arms were getting weaker – I just wasn't strong enough. I looked down and saw that I was too high above the peg to retreat.

With mounting desperation, I swung rightwards and smeared the black rubber of my climbing shoe onto a stretch of sloping rock.

Following with the other foot I was able to pause, almost in balance, as my weight settled onto the rock and the pressure eased out of my arms. And so, suddenly, it was over. *That's it! I've done it! I've done it!* My mind exploded with relief and triumph as I realised I was through the crux. I could breathe again, ablaze in a new-burnished world.

My first VS lead! It had edged my thoughts for months. Was I good enough? Was I strong enough? Would I manage my fear? What would it feel like? And now I was over the hard bit and the rest of the climb would be easy. I'd done it! I was high as a kite driving home that evening, my Honda 50 bouncing along the Calary Bog road from Roundwood. There would be no stopping me now!

In the months that followed I scraped together seven more VS leads, and that meant I was eligible, at last, to join the big boys in the Spillikin Club. The club had never had a female member. With my precious list of climbs, each with the required details of the name, grade, crag, date of the ascent, and name of the second, I went in search of the club secretary. But I was out of luck. Unknown to me, the club had slipped quietly out of existence. Apparently it had been fading away for some time. Emigration and family responsibilities had thinned out the membership, and the heart had been knocked out of the small group with the deaths in the Alps of two young club members, Paul McDermott and Bruce Rodgers, a few years earlier.

Climbing in Ireland was in a lull by 1973/1974, but fortunately I knew most of the active climbers from meeting them in Dalkey or through Tiglin. After getting my mountain-leadership certificate, I had moved seamlessly from being an occasional student in the Tiglin Adventure Centre to being a voluntary mountaineering instructor there. I was twenty-one, and now that I had a qualification, and could lead VS, I was confident in my new role as I introduced soldiers, gardaí and teachers to hill walking and rock climbing.

Weekdays were spent in college and weekends in the centre or away on climbing trips. I was now climbing much more than Bairbre or Sheila and was mixing with the group of experienced Dublin climbers who also volunteered as weekend instructors. They were all male and all a bit older than me, and most of them were single. They seemed interesting.

Life was very exciting all of a sudden, and I felt I had grown up at last. I was climbing well – I was even leading climbs that the great Betty Healy had never attempted – and some of the best climbers in the country were my partners on the crags. I had the world at my feet. Now it was time to test myself in the Alps.

Chapter 5

For over a century, the Chamonix valley below Mont Blanc had been the starting point for countless legendary adventures on rock and ice, and its graveyard was full of famous alpinists. I couldn't wait to go there, but first I had to find a climbing partner.

Nobody seemed to be going to the Alps in that summer of 1974, except Sé Billane, and he had a partner already lined up who was to meet him out there. When I ran into Sé in the pub in Roundwood one Sunday evening, I took a chance and suggested that he and I might meet up in Chamonix and do some acclimatisation routes together before his friend arrived. (If you went straight from sea level onto a high alpine climb, you were almost certain to suffer from headaches and a sick stomach because of the altitude, so most people started the season with an easy climb or two while they adjusted to the thin air.) Sé paused and smiled his slightly mocking smile, and said yes. I was delighted. He had an amusingly dry and intelligent take on life and was always good company. And he was also one of the best climbers around.

I was finished at last with degrees and diplomas and had a permanent teaching job in a primary school near home. There was a great system in national schools then: children moved up to the next class and got their new teacher for the first week of July before the school closed for the summer, so if a class had a newly employed teacher like me, that teacher did one week's work and was then paid for the two-month holiday.

Bairbre and I had won university scholarships based on our Leaving Cert results, and these had given us a small income for the years we were in college. We supplemented this with regular babysitting and had just enough for our day-to-day expenses (we were still living at home) and for weekends away, but now, for the first time, I had real money. And I didn't have to hitchhike anymore. I got a student flight to Paris and a train to Chamonix.

The town was wonderful. There was a mountain at the end of every street, and the glacier running down from Mont Blanc reached almost to the road. Attractive old hotels gave way to fine wooden-clad chalets as I walked out of town to Snell's Field. Snell's Field was the campsite used by all British and Irish climbers. It wasn't a proper campsite or even a proper field, just a level clearing in the forest where there were no facilities and where you didn't have to pay. *Camping sauvage*, the French called it, and that seemed to fit the bill. There was no running water, and people used the surrounding woods as a toilet.

A lot of small tents were pitched randomly around the clearing, and there were a few cars and the odd minivan with a GB registration. Most of the trees at the edge had rough shelters of plastic sheeting strung from their branches, and scattered under them were the litterings of lives lived in the open: plastic café chairs, pots, mugs, blackened fire circles and glinting piles of empty bottles. The sound of the Arve river thundering past, its submerged boulders grinding day and night, was the backdrop to life in Snell's Field.

The place became busy towards evening as people got back from the town or from climbs. The climbers (all men) were easy to spot. They threw off heavy rucksacks, their faces sunburned and lined with tiredness and dehydration. I eyed them with interest: to me they seemed heroic.

The next day I walked up the forest track to Montenvers, the popular viewing spot above the Mer de Glace glacier. The Mer de Glace, a broad and spectacular flow of ice, was ringed by steep mountains, their rock ridges and snowy crests sharp-edged in the sun. I knew I was fit enough for climbing in the Alps, but did I have the psychological strength for this demanding type of mountaineering? I was keen to find out.

When Sé arrived, a few days later, he was my tour guide. In the campsite he'd raise an eyebrow when some climber loped past, and then he'd murmur 'Carrington' or 'Rouse' or 'McIntyre.' If I looked blank at these names, or at 'Venables', 'Renshaw', 'Griffin' or 'the Burgess twins', he would fill me in on their exploits. It took a lot to impress Sé, so I was mightily impressed. These scruffy youths, all long hair and skimpy shorts, were the cream of British mountaineering. They appeared regularly in the climbing magazine *Mountain* and always seemed to be just back from some daring exploit in the Himalayas. They were friendly and low-key, and they cloaked their energy, skill and ambition in casual understatement. They'd go 'up the hill' and reappear a day or two later in the Bar National in Chamonix with hard routes under their belts. These would often be first ascents or first British ascents – achievements that earned them a place in climbing history. Toilet or no toilet, this was the most exciting place I had ever been.

'You know,' said Sé, a few days later, 'there's no such thing as an alpine route that you're not glad to get to the top of.' We were roping up at the foot of our first climb, the North North East Ridge of the Aiguille de l'M, and I was a bit taken aback. Wasn't this alpine climbing meant to be glorious?

In the campsite the previous day we'd shouldered our heavy packs and slogged for hours up a forest path to the foot of the Aiguilles. This jagged array of rocky peaks dominates the town of Chamonix. Up close they are even more dramatic. Sé pointed out the lines of the various climbs that picked their way up the cracks, faces and grooves to the summit pinnacles. From where we stood, any climbers would have looked like ants. Now that the sun had gone, the rock walls looked shadowy, cold and unappealing. I turned away, glad to have the task of sorting out somewhere to sleep to distract me.

Everyone bivouacked the night before a climb. Alpine huts were too expensive, and your tent, home to all the rest of your stuff – the good jeans, the new cheesecloth shirt, the books and the hairbrush –

stayed in the valley. 'This'll do,' said Sé, pointing to a flat spot under a huge boulder. We worked together to heave and roll big stones into a windbreak, and then Sé got meltwater from a nearby snow patch and put a brew on. Tea was always 'a brew'. The light and heat from the little gas stove held the darkness at bay as we waited for the water to boil. Tea, Erin cup-a-soups, bread and cheese – a little shared ritual among the rocks. I kept all my clothes on when I got into my sleeping bag and copied Sé by making a pillow of my boots and rain jacket. I hoped it wouldn't rain.

Of course, if it did rain and was still raining at dawn, we could just pack up and go back to the campsite and not put ourselves through the effort and risk that the next day's climb would bring. But I told myself it would be fine. This was what I'd come for. I wanted to be the little ant-sized climber on the big rock face, and I knew it was a privilege even to be able to attempt it. Throughout the night I listened to the creaking of the nearby Nantillons Glacier and the sporadic crackle of falling rocks. I dozed and woke and looked at the stars.

It was a relief to get going the next morning. The climbing wasn't technically difficult, but wearing a rucksack made it tiring and my heavy alpine boots had none of the flexible adherence of the rock shoes I used at home. Sé led all the pitches, and he was right about being glad to get to the top. This was the shortest route around, but it involved 200 metres of climbing – and then there was the descent. Mountaineers always say that you're only halfway there when you reach the summit, as getting back down safely can take a lot of skill and effort, and most accidents happen on the descent. This one involved abseils, a couloir and a glacier, but it went smoothly enough.

After collecting our sleeping bags from the bivy site, we followed the long toe-bashing path back to the valley floor. As I tramped on down, my mind was full of images of the climb. The hardest pitch was no harder than what I led regularly at home, but it was much more intimidating to encounter such steepness on a long climb. And then there were the bigger peaks just behind the Aiguille de l'M.

We'd had a close-up view of them when we reached the summit and they made our mountain seem puny. Their rearing masses of rock both repelled and enticed me.

When we got back to Snell's Field after the Aiguille de l'M, I was annoyed to hear someone tell Sé that his partner had arrived. Sé had told me a bit about this partner: he was a very keen, strong climber and a member of the Glenfoffany Climbing Club in the Mournes. He'd been living in England for the past five years and had got married there but was now separated. He and Sé and two others had gone on a Himalayan expedition together the previous summer, and he had marched their little team up and down a glacier to celebrate the Twelfth of July.

Glenfoffany antics were all well and good – that club had a wild reputation – but now my precious alpine apprenticeship plans were being sabotaged by this Calvin Torrans bloke who had, inconsiderately, arrived early. He had pitched his tent near our two tents, and he came to meet us. His big smile and easy-going friendliness put me at ease straight away. He wanted to know what I thought of the climb we'd just done – he'd done it too and remembered details of particular pitches. Sé filled him in on who was doing what on the Irish climbing scene (not much), and I was all ears as the talk of climbs and future plans went on into the night.

It was clear that the routes Calvin and Sé had in mind wouldn't accommodate an alpine novice like me, but a friend of Calvin's, Blue, arrived out from England the following day, and as he was in need of a partner it was decided that all four of us would do a climb together. From Montenvers we could see our mountain, the Aiguille du Moine, at the far side of the Mer de Glace glacier. A hut for alpinists, the Refuge du Couvercle, was visible like a doll's house on a shoulder of rock below the peak and we planned to bivouac near it.

When we descended to the Mer de Glace, I was surprised to find that it wasn't white and flat as I had expected but rippled and scaly and grey, cracked with crevasses and scattered with boulders. We zigzagged across it, avoiding the cracks and the meltwater streams that carved runnels into its surface. All the hazards were clearly visible so it was perfectly safe, but it felt surreal to be on this ancient stream of ice, with the occasional crash of an over-balancing boulder as the only hint of its slow creep.

At the far side of the glacier we followed a steep path up to the Couvercle hut, passing some French climbers who were on their way down. They were all men, but they left a cloud of perfumed chemicals in their wake. What sort of mountaineers were these? At home no one ever smelled of anything except the weather and the last bog hole they'd slipped into. On the terrace of the hut there were other well-groomed climbers. With their bright duvet jackets and ironed knee breeches, they looked like extras in a film. Alpine huts with their fees and rules and bustle weren't part of our plan. We had the evening to ourselves as we rolled out our sleeping mats on a patch of flat ground nearby.

That evening, poor Blue was suffering from altitude sickness and throwing up. He hadn't had a chance to acclimatise in the valley. The rest of us were making the most of our airy perch. Calvin and Sé were talking about routes on the Aiguille Verte – a mountain that towered darkly beyond the Moine – and I was watching the moon come up behind the great snowy buttresses of the Grandes Jorasses, the biggest mountain in the chain on the opposite side of the Mer de Glace. I couldn't believe my luck to be high in the Alps and in such company. If Bairbre and Sheila could see me now!

The next day, our climb along the rising crest of the South Ridge was a pleasure from start to finish. The golden granite had handholds and footholds wherever we needed them and we made good time. We descended the 500-metre south face via the Ordinary Route (this is the name always given to the easiest way up). There were a few guided parties on that, people out from the hut, and the guides frowned at us as we down-climbed past them, unroped. Blue, now fully recovered, declared that if I could do a descent like that without a rope, I could do some harder routes with him.

I felt I had wings. This alpine climbing was such fun! I could see Sé and Calvin glissading down the snow slope below – skidding along as if their boots were skis. They'd have tea ready for us at the bivy site when we got down. They were perfect climbing partners: committed, confident mountaineers, each with a great sense of fun.

I loved being in Calvin's company. He wore his climbing experience lightly and was encouraging to me but never patronising. As we crossed back over the Mer de Glace, he and I chatted about people we both knew and climbs we'd both done in Ireland, north and south. At one point we had to cross a gully in the ice, and I lost my footing. He grabbed the ice axe that was tied to the back of my rucksack and saved me from a painful skinning on the rough concrete-like ice – I'd changed to shorts and T-shirt for the afternoon heat. In my diary the next day I wrote that even though I was an independent woman climber, being in occasional need of male support was very nice.

A few days later, Blue and I were queuing for the early-morning cable car – the *téléphérique* – when Blue suddenly hissed, 'Look, it's him, it's Rébuffat!' and cocked his head at a passing climber. We had been waiting in line and watching resentfully as the local guides strode to the front of the queue. They always arrived at the last minute and filled the first cable car, the 6.30 cabin, with their clients. That was their privilege as *guides de montagne*. The clients – rich people who couldn't look after themselves in the mountains – were looked down on by everyone, including me who couldn't look after myself in the mountains.

But here was the man himself, Gaston Rébuffat, familiar from photographs in climbing books and magazines, wearing his customary brown breeches and diamond-patterned knee socks. He had been the first to climb the six great alpine north faces and was one of the best-known climbers in a country that fêtes its climbing heroes. And here we were, on my first visit to the Alps, heading up to do his famous route on the south face of the Midi. It seemed presumptuous.

The spectacular and expensive téléphérique ride felt like cheating. We swung up in the little glass cabin, squashed in with fifty other alpinists, our shadow trailing over the forests, rock walls and serrated peaks above the Chamonix valley until we got to the summit of the

Aiguille du Midi. The cable-car station had been built into the pinnacle of rock at the very top of the mountain – an outrageous feat of engineering that muzzled the slender peak and hollowed it out to provide a high-altitude tourist attraction.

Since its completion in 1955, the téléphérique had proved to be hugely popular with tourists, taking just minutes to whisk them from the valley floor to a height of almost 4,000 metres at the edge of the breathtaking antechamber of Mont Blanc. It was very popular with alpinists too as it gave easy access to the technically difficult rock peaks that were satellites of Mont Blanc. And by depositing its passengers at the top of the mountain, it provided alpinists with a unique starting point.

In the cave-like interior of the station the walkway divides in two – one branch leading to a viewing terrace and café and the other taking the poorly-lit rough-hewn tunnel towards the blinding light of the climbers' exit. We had to put on our goggles to look out at the Vallée Blanche, the greatest expanse of snow I'd ever seen. The snow rolled in blue-shadowed dips and domes up and over Mont Blanc and lapped at the base of dozens of the most famous alpine peaks in the world. The gleaming beauty of the place was dazzling – but, hang on! What were all those climbers doing crunching off in their crampons? We hadn't brought any. My confidence in Blue was a little shaken.

'It'll be fine,' he said and headed jauntily down the narrow snow crest that led precipitously to the bottom of the south face. It couldn't be that hard, I thought. After all, skiers managed it in winter in their big boots. But in winter the ridge of snow is broader and more banked up, and there are rope handrails in place on either side. I found it scary, especially as I didn't even have an ice axe for support. Big steps had been kicked into the snow when it was soft in the heat of the day, but now they formed a frozen staircase of icy scoops, with no banister. Much easier to go up than to go down, and we were going down. They were a bit spaced out too so you had to drop steeply onto each one, taking care not to skid out of it and fall down the slopes that skimmed away towards Chamonix on one side and the Vallée Blanche on the other. But I was damned if I was going to ask Blue for the security of a rope.

The descent turned out to be more of a challenge than the climb. But the climb was hard, a lot harder than the Moine, and my super-stiff boots skittered clumsily on the shiny edges of the granite cracks. Climbers hadn't started using rock shoes on alpine routes yet, and though there were usually pegs to pull on when the climbing got too steep or technical, we always tried to do everything 'free', in a pure style, as we did at home. It was tough going, and there was nowhere to hide from the sun. I hadn't realised how hot it could get, even at almost 4,000 metres.

The climb finished back up at the téléphérique station, and Blue's last belay was on a railing. He had taken a hard variation on the last pitch to bypass some slow climbers, and I needed a tight rope to follow him. When the railing finally came within reach and I began to haul myself over, I saw, beyond Blue's grin, a crowd of tourists with cameras at the ready. They were waiting to see what was being pulled in on the line. I was tired and thirsty and relieved to be finished the climb, but I feigned nonchalance as I got my breath back and untied my ropes in front of the audience. It was the sweetest, if shallowest, pleasure of that first alpine summer.

Another bivouac, another pre-dawn start, and this time it was me suffering from the altitude. My guts were rebelling – maybe it was the gobbets of sickly-sweet Nestlé condensed milk that we had squeezed into our tea at the bivouac.

Blue was sympathetic. 'Did you know,' he said, 'altitude gives you wind?'

Our objective was the North Ridge of the Peigne, a long climb which, according to the guidebook, was one of the finest routes in the Aiguilles. It was graded TD, Très Difficile – the second-from-highest grade of difficulty for an alpine climb – and although the Rébuffat route on the Midi had the same grade, this seemed a lot more serious as it was north-facing and there was no one else in sight all day. The initial pitches were at a low angle, and we gained height steadily, rope length after rope length, but all the while diarrhoea threatened to undo me. Finally we got to a wide ledge and the privacy afforded by some big boulders, and I was able to relieve myself. *I'll be lighter now*, I thought grimly as I looked up at the great dark groove that reared up for 200 metres above us.

Blue set off confidently, and I followed as quickly as I could when he pulled the rope in. But there was nothing quick about our ascent. Corner followed corner, each steeper than the last, and there was no respite. Blue motored on, and when my turn came to second him, always too soon, I pulled and wriggled and hauled myself up cracks and onto ledges and up more cracks and corners until my arms were cramping with fatigue.

And still there was more to come. It was late afternoon when we got out into the sun amid the beautiful rocky spires of the Aiguilles. There was no time to hang around – we had to find the top of the Ordinary Route and then move quickly if we were to make it down to the glacier before dark. We were tired, and the descent was long, steep and complicated. From one little col we scrambled easily down a couloir and suddenly came to a steep drop. No chance of down-climbing that and no abseil anchor either. We could set up our own anchor of course, but that would mean taking the risk that the first person to abseil might end up spinning slowly in space below an overhang, having got to the end of the rope but with no rock within reach. No, no choice but to traipse back up to the ridge and scout around for another way down, for a peg in a crack, a sweet paper or a cigarette butt, some sign that other people had squeezed through that gap or stepped carefully along that ledge to reach the easier rock below.

We got down to the glacier, to the relief of there being nowhere further to fall, just as full darkness came. No need to rush now. We descended to the tree line and the start of the twisting forest path and as we trudged along its zigzags by head torch, the lights of Chamonix flickered through the trees, confusing us about how much further we had to go. By the time we got back to our tents, we'd been on the move almost non-stop for eighteen hours.

'Dépêchez-vous! Vite, vite!' growled the concierge, as I was inspecting my bruised knees in the municipal showers in Chamonix the following day. I'd woken up aching all over but thrilled to have put in such a day. And I was very glad to be back in the undemanding safety of the ordinary world. The public showers with their concrete floors and brick walls were uninviting, but the water was hot, and for a few francs you could wash yourself and all your sweaty clothes before the elderly concierge came banging on the door.

As far as the Chamonix shopkeepers and café owners were concerned, English-speaking climbers were thieves. You couldn't blame the business people: climbers saw café chairs as fair game, and you might meet a friend in the little supermarket who couldn't stop for a chat because he had frozen food stuck down his jeans. But Snell Sports was off-limits. Not only did Mr Snell allow free use of his field but he kept an unofficial postbox just inside the door of his sports shop. For years my summer address was 'c/o Snell Sports, Chamonix'.

Maurice, the owner of the Bar Nash, stood behind the counter and surveyed the English and Irish climbers with his one good eye. He passed no comment and never smiled. It was standing room only every night as we drank sour vin rouge from little tumblers while the Rolling Stones wailed about 'Angie' on the jukebox. Sé said there was a real Angie who had broken some climber's heart.

A few of the English climbers had girls with them – they were invariably fair-haired and pretty – but in general it looked as if the girlfriends had stayed at home. None of the other girls in the campsite seemed to be doing any climbing, even though the weather was perfect. They spent their days sunbathing. I was delighted one day when Sé called me the *alpiniste extraordinaire* – or was he slagging? He had his head bent over his Primus stove and I couldn't read his grin. It was a great first season for me. In just two weeks I had climbed four classic climbs. But I had only led the easy pitches on all of them, and that would have to change.

Calvin cooked for our little group every evening, and other people often dropped by for a chat. He knew everyone. I was fascinated by him, by his energy and warmth and constant good humour. He seemed so at ease with life – no fear of him losing any sleep over the Meaning of Meaning. I was struck too by how much he loved climbing and how he enjoyed every aspect of it: the planning, the preparation of the gear, the graceful movement on rock and ice. Cliffs and mountains were his medium, and he was more at home on them than any climber I'd ever met.

I was watching him across the campfire one evening when he caught my eye and grinned. Oh God, was there any chance he'd fall for me? I knew he liked me and by now I was head over heels in love with him. Before I left, he said I should climb at Fairhead. Me, at Fairhead? That cliff on the north Antrim coast had a fearsome reputation. It sounded more challenging than the Alps. He said it wasn't that hard, that climbing hard grades was mainly psychological and that we should climb together there when he got back to Belfast in the autumn.

I was only just getting to know him and hated to be going home. He was never out of my thoughts from then on.

Chapter 6

In September I got a lift up to the Mournes with some Dublin climbers. We would be staying in the Glenfoffany Climbing Club hut for the weekend but stopped off in the Wilmar House bar – the club's 'local' – in nearby Newcastle to see who was around. I was hoping against hope that Calvin would be there.

The place was packed, all loud voices and cigarette smoke, and then I spotted him, in the middle of a group as always. He was wearing a bright purple shirt with a long looped collar, a shirt that must already have been out of fashion when he'd left it behind in his mother's house years before. But what did I care? He was gorgeous anyway, and his big smile was just for me.

From then on we spent as much time as we could together, and our relationship was well established when we set off for Fairhead a few weeks later. The weather didn't look very promising, but as we drove north from Dublin Calvin proclaimed, with a Paisley boom, that we'd soon leave 'the grey skies of the Irish Republic for the blue skies of a Free Ulster!'

He was right. By the time we got to Ballycastle on the north Antrim coast, the seafront was cheerful in the sunshine and Scotland seemed dreamily close, just beyond Rathlin Island. Fairhead, still 8 kilometres away, was clearly visible: a cliff with the heft of a mountain, its impressive profile marking the north-east turn of the coast of Ireland. We approached the crag along the top, and even though

I was expecting it, I was shocked by the abrupt 100-metre drop of its rock face. There were wide vertical walls split by thin cracks and bounded by huge corners.

Calvin pointed out the two climbs that had been done at this western end – Hell's Kitchen and Equinox – both with bulging overhangs near the top, and he talked about other possible climbable 'lines'. To me it all looked intimidating, and much of it was as grim and inhospitable as those unloved corners of the Alps that never make it onto postcards.

There were only twenty climbs on the cliff at that time, late 1974, and most of the rest were grouped around the Greyman's Path descent gully at the far end. When we scrambled down the Greyman's, Calvin showed me the line of Njold's Saga, a fierce-looking climb he'd put up (made the first ascent of) the previous year. It took a dramatic rising traverse across a series of massive columns and finished up behind a towering pinnacle.

The monstrous Gothic architecture of the rock seemed to leave no room for the sky. I couldn't see myself ever leading climbs in this place. The weather deteriorated, and it was soon too wet to climb, but that trip north set the pattern that was to be at the core of our shared lives from then on. The sequence was always the same: checking the weather and deciding where to go; spending Saturday and Sunday on the cliffs; and then, as the sensations and emotions of that began to settle into memories, chatting about it all on the way home and looking forward to the next weekend.

In the following months, on steep rock faces and over long drives, I got to know the man I had fallen in love with. From the stories he told me about growing up in the loyalist working-class enclave of Belfast's Shankill Road, I realised that his background could hardly have been more different from mine. But when he went on to describe the impulses that had channelled him into climbing, I could see that the emotional draw of the mountains had been just the same for both of us.

When I first met Calvin I used to wonder how he could get such uncomplicated joy from life. Had he worked out the answers to the big questions that I'd been mulling over for years? Then I realised that he didn't have any of the answers. He just knew that there were no answers, and through climbing he had found a way to live well without needing to search for higher truths. He had an instinctive suspicion of all ideologies and belief systems, and the sectarianism he had witnessed as a child further discredited organised religion for him. His brushes with Protestantism as a belief system had been superficial, and the influences it had left were purely cultural.

The Torranses were Protestants who had come over from Scotland in some previous generation, but they didn't darken the door of their local Church of Ireland church other than for baptisms, marriages and funerals. Neither did any of their neighbours. Churchgoing was strictly for the middle classes. The children did go to the Zion Tabernacle Sunday School where evangelical young women taught them the basics of prayers, hymns and the Bible.

The family were never involved in politics. Calvin's grandfather was the Grand Master of an Orange Lodge, but his father, a quiet temperate man, would have nothing to do with the conservative 'Protestants first' principles of Orangeism. There was a day in the mid 1950s when Ian Paisley had come to neighbouring Percy Street to canvass for a local Unionist election candidate. At that time Paisley was a fiery young evangelical preacher who was making a name for himself as a populist politician. He stopped at a place that locals called Blitz Square – one of the sites that had been bombed out during the war – and a crowd gathered. Calvin and his mate Tommy stopped to listen.

'Look at those Catholics down there on the Falls,' bellowed the preacher, pointing at the nearby streets. 'You don't even have to look at them – you can smell them!'

'That's not right,' said Tommy to Calvin. 'He's a Christian minister – he shouldn't be saying things like that.' Calvin said nothing, but now that he thought about it he knew that Tommy was right. Lots of people said things like that about the Catholics but a Christian minister should never say the like of that.

Religion was tribal in the North, but the Shankill was adjacent to the Catholic stronghold of the Falls Road, and there was a lot of contact between the two communities before the Troubles broke out. Every morning thousands of workers from both areas would flow together through the gates of the big linen mills on the Blackstaff River. In the mills people generally preferred to work 'with their own kind', but relations were easy-going and mixed marriages were not uncommon.

The Victorian mill workers' houses where Calvin and his family lived were 'two-up two-down': two bedrooms upstairs and a kitchen and living room downstairs, with an outside toilet in the backyard. The house had been condemned as substandard well before Calvin was born there in 1943. Everyone in his family always worked, once they were old enough (fourteen), and they always worked in the linen mill. While he was still at school, both of his parents and his three older siblings were all bringing home wages from the mill, but his mother still struggled to make ends meet. Mrs Torrans had two priorities: food on the table and clean clothes on the children. Like many of the women in the Shankill, she depended on the pawnshop and the moneylender to tide her over from week to week.

The stories that Calvin told me about his childhood seemed like scenes from a picaresque novel. He and his pals spent their waking hours, outside of school time, playing football in the street and running wild. They found constant excitement hopping lorries, scaling high walls and breaking into forbidden premises. There were injuries in their group, and even deaths, but that was no deterrent.

They had various ways of making money. You'd get paid for collecting glass bottles and jars and bringing them back to the local shop. Or you could collect skins for Sam the Skinman. Skins were the peelings off vegetables and potatoes, and you could go around to the neighbours to collect them and sell them on to Sam who had a pig yard. He'd give you sixpence for a bucketful, or lend you a big black pram and pay one and six (a shilling and sixpence) for the fill of it. Some of the women would keep their skins for an older lad who was a bit soft in the head, but if you timed it right you could steal some of the skins off the back of his handcart.

I was surprised how often Calvin went to the cinema. In Bantry we went once or twice a year, but he and his mates went once or twice a week, and at the Diamond – everyone called it the Swamp – you could pay in with jam jars. Confrontations with Catholic street gangs, often armed with hurleys, were a hazard as he got older, and the cinema was one place where you needed to be very careful. If you went to Clonard cinema in the (Catholic) Falls, you had to get up and leave before the end in case you were spotted. When it came to their own cinema, the Stadium, Calvin and his friends gave as good as they got. They'd move down to the back before the end of the film and watch out for anyone who didn't stand for 'God Save the Queen'. Then they'd surround them and give them a good thumping before they could make it to the door.

The only good thing about school was the football at break time. Stan, Calvin's teacher for his last two years, was a brute, and Calvin mitched, on and off. Sometimes his mother would keep him at home to do the messages and he'd be the one left in the house to answer the door when the moneylender made his weekly call to collect his payments. 'Ah, sorry, Mr Sandler, me ma will have it for you next week.' But mitching was a risky business and you had to keep a sharp eye out for the truancy man on his bicycle. Mrs Torrans was summoned twice when Calvin was caught skipping school, but another woman went to court for her because she herself couldn't read or write. Calvin's mate, Albert Glover, was caught once too often and was sent to borstal for two years.

Calvin loved to get out of Belfast, especially on Sundays when a pall of Puritan gloom would settle over the city. All of the swings in all of the public parks were tied up by the council workers, and he knew one woman who took the little swing out of her budgie's cage and covered the small mirror with a cloth, out of respect for the Sabbath. But down at Gresham Street bus station there would be a holiday air as groups of men and boys gathered for a day out in the country, a day that they'd dedicate to hunting and fishing.

There was a tradition of hunting in Calvin's family and he often went out with his Uncle Jamesie who brought his ferrets along in a box. A favourite place for hunting rabbits was around the half-buried air-raid shelters near Nutts Corner airport. The ground was riddled with burrows, and Calvin and his mates would cover all the holes of a burrow with nets before letting a muzzled ferret loose into one of the tunnels. When the rabbits bolted for daylight they got caught in the nets, and the boys finished them off with the whack of a stick. You'd get half a crown for a rabbit at a shop in the Shankill, but the money was by the by – the adventure of the day out was the main thing.

When Calvin joined the Boys' Brigade at the age of twelve, he began to see the world beyond Belfast. He signed up for the Boys' Brigade because they brought you away for two weeks' holidays in the summer. It was like the Boy Scouts and was interdenominational, though all the denominations were Protestant. The boys had to wear a military-style uniform with a white sash and a pillbox hat, and there was a lot of marching and praying and hymn-singing, but it was worth it for the holidays. In the summer the leaders brought them away to Scotland or the Isle of Man where they slept in church halls on sewn-up flour bags filled with straw. They learned skills like map-reading, though that was only ever done indoors, and heard about activities like youth-hostelling – something they'd never have heard about at home.

Calvin's hostel card was his key to a new life. He had first seen the Mourne Mountains on a Sunday school trip to Newcastle a few years earlier, and the dramatic rise and roll of them had taken his breath away. Now, thanks to his hostel card, he was able to spend every weekend in the Mournes and for a boy from the backstreets of Belfast – a lone youngster exploring them on foot – the new landscapes were vast, wild and exhilarating. He'd follow an old mine track or a little sandy path into the heart of the range and then take off over the rising heathery ground towards one of the rocky summits in the distance. From the top there would be a new stretch of land to view, another deepening river valley with its unique tapestry of bog and rock.

In bad weather the mountain summits could be eerie places. They were scattered with tors – dramatic granite domes and towers whose dark bulk seemed to grow in size and menace when the wind rose and the mist swirled around them. This never bothered Calvin, and images of the rain-lashed tors would flicker through his mind during the weekdays back in Belfast.

Every Friday evening he would hitch down to Newcastle, the town on the northern edge of the Mournes, and stay in the youth hostel there. The following morning he'd set out to walk across the mountains to one of the other hostels, and on Sundays he'd take a different route back to Newcastle before hitching home. He was always on his own and rarely met another soul in the hills, but he found his way easily enough. He had a map, and if he did get a bit lost the big granite-block Mourne Wall that ran over many of the summits was a good reference point.

He bought milk and bread in the small shops around the Mournes and sometimes ate turnips that had been left out in the fields for the sheep. It wasn't until he was fourteen, and working full-time, that he could afford proper food. 'Hey big spender,' mocked a beefy hosteller who noticed him buying just a single egg.

The summer before he left school, Calvin spent a season working as a potato picker. Tatie-picking, he told me, was back-breaking work, but the money – fourteen shillings a day – was good. He gave most of what he earned to his mother, and the rest went on his weekend trips where it paid for his hostel overnights. He spent fifteen shillings on a second-hand A-framed 'Commando' rucksack, but coming back through the Shankill on a Sunday night he'd have to slip the rucksack off and carry it under his arm. Otherwise there'd be a gang of children behind him singing, 'Oh, I love to go a-wandering' all the way to his house in Urney Street.

The people he met in the hostels were all older and mainly middle-class. They were friendly, and they talked about other hostels they'd stayed in, places he'd read about in the hostellers' handbook. He bought a copy of the An Óige handbook too, the one for the Republic, and when he was still just thirteen (and looking like a skinny eleven-year-old) he set off on his own to hitch around what most Northerners still called 'the Free State'.

Like me, over a decade later, Calvin could afford to travel because he hitchhiked and used the cheap accommodation that youth hostels provided. The welcoming triangular hostel symbol hung above the front door of converted farm buildings, town houses, coastguard barracks, and even the odd castle, in all corners of the island. And, like me, once he left home he was intent on crossing the nearest border and setting foot in another country. But instead of travelling in the slip-stream of a confident older sister, he was doing it on his own.

As he made his way down the west coast of Ireland in the summer of 1956, the exotic stamps built up in his hostel card: Bunnaton, Trá na Rosann, Galway. He lived on bread and cheese, and the overnight fee was his big expense. He had to doss down in a field near Lough Derg one night when he didn't make it to the hostel, but he had his sleeping bag with him and found that it was no great ordeal.

Another night, on Achill Island, a farmer agreed to let him stay in his barn but came back out a few minutes later to invite him into the house. 'Come on in, sure aren't you one of our own.' One of our own? Did he mean 'We're all Irish anyway' or did he think that a Northerner choosing to come south must be a Catholic? Hardly, with a name like Calvin. He was to sleep on the floor of the son's room. The boy was doing his homework in the warm kitchen, and the radio was on. The programme being broadcast was in Irish, and it was Calvin's first time to hear the language being spoken. When he got as far as Killarney he had to ask for directions to the hostel. He approached a group of jarvies, the drivers of horse-drawn jaunting cars who were waiting to ferry tourists up to the Gap of Dunloe. The jarvies sized him up, perplexed, and then one of them took his pipe from his mouth and declared, 'I think he's German.'

In Belfast, Calvin's house was just two minutes' walk from Greeves's mill, and it was there that he went to work on his fourteenth birthday, in 1957. Greeves's dated from the 1850s, and little had changed over the years except that now the red brick of the six-storey mills and the maze of workers' houses below them was dulled by a hundred years of grime. The wage in the mill was £2.10 a week, and Calvin handed most of that up 'for the house'.

The working conditions were Dickensian. The main spinning room was a thunderous vault where the workers had to lip-read because of the noise. The tiled floor was kept constantly wet so that the linen fibres didn't dry out, and everyone worked in their bare feet. Calvin did various jobs in the mill, and his task as a band-tier was the most difficult. It involved risking his fingers to do running repairs on the spinning machines. These were giant machines with hundreds of moving parts and they were never turned off. But he wasn't concerned about his fingers; his worry was the spinner standing behind him who'd give him a clatter on the back of the head if he messed up her machine.

At other times he was sent to help the weavers on an upper floor. Some of these women were on piecework – they were paid according to the amount they produced. One of them, a Catholic who used to work non-stop all day, would scatter holy water all around her loom and often sent Calvin to Clonard chapel to get her bottle of holy water refilled. He knew where to go – he and his mates used dare each other to run in and pee in the holy-water font at Clonard chapel.

He wasn't long in the mill when the foreman asked him to take up an apprenticeship. He got the offer for three reasons: he was male, he was showing skill as a worker, and he was a Protestant. He turned it down. It would have meant never being free on Saturdays and having to give up his weekends in the Mournes.

He never tired of the Mournes. No two days there were ever the same: the vegetation and the wildlife varied with the seasons, and the weather varied by the hour. Then, one weekend in 1957, when he was fourteen, he got a chance that was to change his life. There were granite cliffs scattered around the mountains, cliffs that he'd been skirting for the previous few years but that he'd have loved to climb, had he known how. He'd seen climbers in the distance once or twice but hadn't been able to talk to them.

Then came his lucky break. He happened to be at the new Kinnahalla youth hostel on the southern side of the Mournes on the day of its official opening, and among the crowd of dignitaries and hostellers he met a man who had all the gear for rock climbing – a rope, slings, pegs and a peg hammer – but no partner. The two of them went to Hen Mountain where they climbed the route 'Fingerbowl'. Calvin found it easy and wanted to do more, but his partner was happy with just the one climb. It was to be five years before he had the chance to climb again, but the intensity of the experience stayed with him. Rock climbing, with its powerful combination of mental focus and precise athletic movement, had immediate and deep appeal for him.

Just as everyone in working-class Belfast left school on their fourteenth birthday, so every male went to the British Army recruiting office on the day they turned seventeen. Prospects for advancement in the mill were low, especially with the collapse of the linen market in 1960, and it was hard to get into the shipyard if you didn't have contacts. The only other option was emigration, but you needed money for that.

The Catholic lads from Carrick Hill and the Falls Road all joined the British Army too, and the Royal Irish Fusiliers was everyone's regiment of choice. Young men who had squared up to each other in the streets not long before now found that the fire had gone out of their sectarian animosities, and they all got on very well together as new recruits. They were sent to Derry for twelve weeks of basic training and then shipped out to an army camp in Tripoli, Libya.

King Idris of Libya was a British ally at the time, and, in this decade before Colonel Gaddafi's coup, the country was at peace. Kitted out in their regulation khaki shorts and wide-brimmed hats, Calvin and his mates began to get their bearings in North Africa. The routines of daily life were much the same in every army camp, but here on the edge of the desert there was a palm-fringed beach to swim at and an ancient Arab city to explore.

Calvin got opportunities in the army that he would never have got at home. He learned to drive and was a member of a trophy-winning athletics team. He had athletes' blood: his father boxed and three of his grand-uncles had been founder members of Linfield, the very successful Belfast football club. In the army he trained and qualified as a coach in judo and in basketball, and was able to spend most of his time in a tracksuit instead of a uniform.

When he was twenty-one, after a further posting to northern Germany, he was given the option of returning to Belfast to work as a sports instructor with the army youth team. He couldn't have wished for more. This was his chance to go back to the Mournes to walk and climb, and he would be able to bring others out into the mountains as part of his working day.

Now that he was out regularly in the craggy hills, he began to meet other climbers. Like him they were chancing their arm by scrambling up easy stuff in their walking boots, with white nylon ropes tied around their waists. For protection they hammered pegs into cracks as they climbed, or jammed other gadgets in by hand: wooden wedges, industrial screw nuts or even stones of different sizes – whatever could be bunged securely into a crack and have a sling anchored to it. The sling, a sewn loop of strong webbing, was what you clipped your rope to as you climbed – if you fell it would hold your weight while your partner hung onto the rope from below. Steel karabiners were used to clip the rope to the sling and once your rope was running through the karabiner, you could relax a little.

A good 'runner' was a god-send – you might be hanging on for dear life with one hand and fumbling to place gear with the other as your strength ebbed and a fall yawned below you, but then, rope clipped, it all became manageable again: the handholds looked bigger and the next moves easier as your racing heart slowed down – if you fell now you wouldn't go far.

At that time, in the 1960s, climbers rarely fell because they almost always climbed at a standard of difficulty that was well within their range of competence. Anything else would have been foolhardy given their primitive protection. The golden rule was the same one that I was to hear six or seven years later: the leader should never fall.

In 1965, the army sent Calvin to work at an Outward Bound centre in England, to broaden his experience as a mountaineering instructor. It was only for a month, but it was in the Lake District, the heart of the thriving English climbing scene, and it made a big impression on him. The instructors were all experienced climbers and the talk was of routes and grades and of the new lightweight aluminium gear that was being designed specifically for climbing. He came home with a new perspective on what might be possible on rock.

Before the days of mobile phones and social media, climbing clubs filled a very important function. The strong social scene they provided revolved around midweek get-togethers in pubs. This was where the weekend's climbing was planned with a partner and lifts arranged to a club hut in the mountains. It was Calvin's good luck that a new club had recently been formed in the Mournes. The Glenfoffany Climbing Club was an irreverent, exuberant working-class group whose unruly members escaped to the mountains every weekend to indulge their enthusiasm for rock climbing. It was a perfect fit for him, unlike the well-established upper-middle-class Irish Mountaineering Club, which he found to be stuffy and unfriendly.

Glenfoffany Climbing Club members were very active 'new routers'. When they took to the crags it was often to climb where no one had ever set foot, or hand, before. For three or four years towards the end of the 1960s they explored the cliffs in the Mournes and put up new routes at a rate not previously seen in Ireland. Then they wrote detailed descriptions of where exactly they'd gone on the hitherto virgin rock so that other climbers could repeat their climbs.

Calvin climbed his first new route by accident. Calvert Moore, a founder member of Glenfoffany, had his eye on a possible line at Lower Cove in the Mournes, but when he uncoiled his rope at the foot of the cliff and took another look at the rock above, he decided he'd be content to fill the no-risk role of 'second' and handed the end of the rope to Calvin with a casual 'Here ye go.' And so Calvin did his first new route, challenging himself on rock that nobody had ever climbed before and revelling in the heightened commitment demanded by that new experience. He had recently finished his six years in the army, and he called the climb 'Demob'. Climbed in February 1967, it was to be the first of his hundreds of new routes.

Climbing a new route is something special. It is an act of creation. Where there has just been rock the lead climber now unveils a finished piece, an invisible sequence that he (or she) has traced in stone from earth to sky, its pathway discernible for the first time. For example, 'up the left-hand groove . . . follow the thin crack to the ledge . . . step right.' As lead climber it is yours to describe, yours to grade in terms of difficulty and yours to name. It is yours forever. Descriptions of climbs in particular areas are collected and published in guidebooks by individuals, clubs or national representative bodies. They serve the dual purpose of providing information for visiting climbers and preserving a record of the climbing history of the various cliffs.

As a 'first ascensionist', your name, and that of your partner, will appear beside the description of your climb. It is a formal recognition of your contribution to climbing history. First ascensionists have the privilege of naming their climbs, and they're free to call them anything they like. The generation of climbers who were active in the 1940s and 1950s often incorporated relevant rock features like buttresses, grooves or gullies into their route names, but from the 1960s on the choices tended to tell more about the climbers than the climbs. Some, like 'Hell's Kitchen' and 'Hurricane', reflected a route's difficulty or seriousness. Others were favourite song titles or quirky wordplays, and still others – especially if they involved damp cracks – were amusing double entendres. I didn't think they were a bit amusing.

At around this time the Glenfoffany climbers became aware of a group of strong young Dubliners who had also formed a new climbing club. They were working-class lads too, and their passion for mountaineering had grown in the wilds of Wicklow. Their gateway had been through the Boy Scouts, and, as with Calvin, the network of youth hostels that were scattered, a day's walk apart, throughout the mountains.

The Spillikin Club, which was to have such mythic status for me as a novice climber, was a club for elite climbers only as you had to lead climbs graded Very Severe or above to be eligible to join. In the 1960s, Very Severe was the level of difficulty being tackled by the top climbers of the day, and there was only a handful of harder rock routes anywhere in the country.

The Spillikin climbers were all alpinists for whom rock climbing in Ireland was seen as training for the big peaks. Membership never went above twenty, but its raw energy and burning ambition soon attracted the most able climbers from both sides of the border, Calvin included. This new concentration of strong climbers and the inevitable dynamics of male competition – there were no female members – coincided with what was to be a momentous discovery for Irish climbing: the possibilities of the great sea cliff of Fairhead in County Antrim.

Calvert Moore had been shown photographs of Fairhead by an English climber who had kayaked along that corner of the north-east coast. Moore immediately recognised the potential of the big basalt sea cliff and persuaded the Spillikin Club to have an exploratory meet there at Easter in 1967. He booked the fisherman's cottage down by the shore in Murlough Bay at the eastern end of the cliff, and it was roomy enough for the dozen or so climbers from Northern Ireland and the Republic who turned up on the Friday night.

The next morning they left the cottage in high spirits and headed for a big prow of rock that cut into the sky a few kilometres away. As they came closer they had to pick their way through a jumble of big boulders, eyes down as they avoided holes hidden beneath the heather and bracken. Then they topped a rise and were suddenly confronted by the mighty cliff. It stretched before them in an unbroken curtain of rock that filled a wide bay. It was hard to judge its height but there was no doubting its steepness. The geometry of the cliff was stark and unfamiliar. Smooth vertical walls alternated with straight cracks, columns and corners. None of it leaned back, but there were sharp black juts here and there that the newcomers realised must be sizeable overhangs. How could you climb that?

Calvin and the others were used to launching up easier-angled rock, armed with the few bits of basic gear that were available at the time: a couple of pegs, slings, a peg hammer, and maybe a Moac. The Moac, a one-inch aluminium wedge, was their biggest piece of protection, but these cracks were wider than any Moac, and they went on for a hundred metres. The climbers could see they weren't ready for this.

Dwarfed and intimidated, they realised now that the crags they usually climbed on – Glendalough and Luggala in Wicklow, Slieve Beg in the Mournes and the big mountain cliffs of Donegal – were friendly places. This dark north-facing bastion would never be friendly. They walked on, craning to scan each new section as it towered into view above them. Eventually they came to a break in the rampart of rock, a grassy gully that led easily to the top. Even this, the Greyman's Path, had its own gloomy atmosphere. The gully narrowed as it rose between black walls and sentinel pinnacles, and when they scrambled up the last steepening, they found themselves in the shadow of a huge pillar, an ominously perched column that had toppled to form a bridge over the rocky exit gap.

There were sporadic visits to 'the Head' from Spillikin Club members in the late 1960s, and some first ascents of note were done by Paul McHugh. This gifted Dubliner dared to get to grips with the intimidating cracks and corners and produced half a dozen lines that far outclassed any of the routes that existed in Ireland up till then. But it wasn't until the 1970s that the mighty cliff came to be climbed on regularly. And the climbers who climbed on it most often were Calvin and me.

Calvin was twenty-three when he left the British Army in 1966 – just a few short years before it became a toxic presence in the North due to the Troubles. He was able to walk straight into a relatively good job in the post office in Belfast because employment with the British postal service was reserved for ex-servicemen. On his first day at the post office he was told to collect his bike in the yard, but before he could set out on his delivery he had to find one of his mates to teach him how to cycle it. He had driven heavy tanks and big trucks in the army, but he'd never had access to a bicycle before.

At around this time he started going out with a young Englishwoman he'd met in the Glenfoffany Climbing Club. Marsha was training to be a teacher, and when she qualified they moved to her home place of Hartlepool, in England, where they married. He continued to work as a postman in Hartlepool, climbing whenever he could. When he and Marsha moved to Kendal in the Lake District he met people for whom, like him, work was just a way of financing climbing, and weekends were for adventurous trips to North Wales or to Scotland. He built up valuable experience to complement his natural talent, and the variety of cliffs he climbed on in England and Wales opened his eyes to the possibilities of Fairhead and other crags back home.

Back in the 1960s and 1970s, the natural progression for climbers was to move to ever bigger cliffs and mountains. After an apprenticeship on rock, people learned how to use ice axes and crampons while winter climbing in Scotland and then headed to the Alps. Calvin had four good summer seasons based in Chamonix, in the French Alps, before being invited on a trip to the Himalayas in 1973.

It was a small team, all from the Spillikin Club, and they chose unclimbed peaks above the Kullu Valley in northern India as their objective. The trip was a complete failure: they had sent their equipment on ahead by boat, but it never arrived, and all they could do was view the mountains from a distance. Things weren't going too well at home either, and Calvin and Marsha separated later that year.

Chapter 7

The Troubles were full blown in the North in 1974, when Calvin came back to live in Belfast, after we'd first met in Chamonix. He had two things on his mind (apart from me): getting a job and climbing new routes at Fairhead. He got work with a building firm, some of it on new sites and some clearing up after bomb blasts. New undercurrents of violence were surfacing all the time. The people you encountered in the street, in the bank, or in the workplace could be paramilitaries from either side.

One day he was going into a chemist's shop on Donegall Road when two men and a woman came rushing out, apologising as they pushed past him. Inside, the shocked assistant told him that they had just planted a bomb. Without a thought he chased after the trio but didn't catch them. The shop was vacated and blew up shortly afterwards.

Friends of friends were shot or kneecapped or their workplaces bombed. You had to know what streets, taxis and pubs were safe, and when not to open your mouth. Every trip into the city involved security checks before you could enter certain streets, cafés and shops, and time and again there were evacuations of buildings because of bomb scares.

At a later stage of the Troubles, a climbing friend of ours was caught up in one of the countless incidents that traumatised so many Northerners over the three decades. 'I was in the wrong place at the wrong time,' he said and told us how he and his apprentice had been on their way to work when they were randomly targeted by, he guessed, dissident Republican paramilitaries.

They had stopped at traffic lights in the city when two armed men suddenly appeared at the door of their van. The men took the apprentice hostage and put a bomb into the van before ordering our friend to drive it to a nearby British Army checkpoint. They would then detonate it remotely. Our friend told us about the terror he felt as he drove. 'It was like soloing a hard Extreme way above the ground,' he said. 'You've no rope and every move is really desperate and you think you're going to fall any minute.' He described how he drove towards the checkpoint, desperately weighing up his options as he came closer to the armed soldiers. Then, decision made, he swerved the van up onto the central reservation, jumped out, shouted a warning, and ran. The bomb didn't go off, the soldiers didn't shoot, and his apprentice was released unharmed.

With me working in Dublin and Calvin in Belfast, we could only meet at weekends. Arrangements were hard to make and harder to keep. Our phone at home was in the kitchen, and there could be up to eight members of my family around when someone yelled, 'Clare, Calvin's on the phone.' That was if he could find a public phone that wasn't bust or bombed and if he had the right change for the operator. He lodged with his niece but she didn't have a phone so I had to ring her neighbour when I wanted to talk to him.

I took the train to Belfast most Friday evenings, and there were times when the city centre outside Great Victoria Street station was a chaos of sirens and diversions. I didn't feel particularly at risk. After all, Calvin and the other Glenfoffany climbers were living with this every day of the week. But there were times when it seemed that bombs were going off all over the place. Sometimes the blast and flash were just a street away as we drove north out of the city towards the silence and darkness of Fairhead.

Sometimes the train didn't run because of bomb scares or damage to the line, and on those occasions Calvin would drive down, but his car gave trouble on and off and there were often long delays at the many British Army or RUC checkpoints. There were sporadic petrol shortages too, though that was part of a general fuel crisis and had nothing to do with the Troubles.

Calvin could tell by the look of someone whether he was a Fenian (Catholic) or a Prod (Protestant). He knew by a person's features and colouring, and he assured me that I looked like a Fenian. It was a skill he shared with many Northerners, and presumptions about religious and cultural affiliations were further confirmed on hearing someone's surname or where they'd grown up. But that never mattered among climbers. No one brought tribal politics to the crag or to the pub, or to Glenfoffany. Most Belfast climbers went to the Mournes every weekend to get away from the tension; we always drove on up to Fairhead. Few other southern climbers ventured north during the 1970s.

I didn't like Tuesdays or Wednesdays at school because I had an extra chore in the afternoons: I had to take senior classes for sewing. This was for the last hour of the school day when my own forty-five senior infants had gone home, and I longed to be left in my empty classroom to crawl under tables after wayward crayons while I tried to remember who I was and why I had decided to become a teacher.

Teaching sewing single-handed to a big group of boys and girls is torture, even if you start with all the needles threaded and a knot in every thread. But once Wednesday sewing was over it felt as if it was almost the weekend. And now I had company on the train to Belfast because Sé Billane, who worked in Dublin as a goldsmith and with whom I'd climbed in the Alps, had started going out with Valerie MacCartney, a friend of mine from Glenfoffany.

During our first winter together, Calvin and I spent almost every weekend at Fairhead. The cliff faces out to Scotland over the wild Sea of Moyle, and in stormy weather the wind whips around it from every direction. Fierce squalls race in from Rathlin Island and conjure up an atmosphere of mythic struggle. Giants, ghosts, bewitched swan-children and even dragons have found a place here.

Back from the edge, the heathery land slopes down to Lough na Cranagh, a lake with a fortified island, or crannóg, dating from the

Iron Age, the stones of its curved retaining wall still visible above the waterline. We had our own place of refuge nearby: a little cottage with a half door and thick whitewashed walls. When it was too stormy even to walk below the cliff, we'd light a fire in the big hearth and listen to Carole King, Neil Young and Leonard Cohen on Calvin's battery-powered cassette player while the wind lashed the sycamores out the back.

The cottage was one of a succession of old empty buildings near the headland that local farmers let us use as climbers' huts. They never took any money from us, and though the Troubles persisted for another twenty-five miserable years, they never inquired as to the politics or religion of the trickle of climbers, from either side of the border, who came up at weekends.

English visitors were few. Very occasionally we'd meet two or three climbers at the top of the cliff – young men with English accents – who would return our greeting but keep walking. They were British Army soldiers, Calvin would tell me. 'Didn't you notice their haircuts?' The soldiers always kept a very low profile.

Sé and Valerie often came and shared the hut with us, and the four of us climbed throughout that winter on a low outlier of the main cliff. This 'Small Crag' had never been climbed on and was much less intimidating than the main cliff. I'd done a few first ascents before – long, easy lines on scattered mountain crags in the west of Ireland – but now I learned to scan virgin rock and pick out feasible lines to clean.

Cleaning a line involved abseiling down it to clear loose rock, mud and bits of vegetation before attempting to climb it. All four of us put in a lot of effort and we each came away with climbs we were proud of, climbs whose details appeared in the new *Antrim Coast* rock-climbing guidebook that was published the following year.

By the spring of 1975 I had led a lot of Very Severe and some Hard Very Severe climbs at other crags, and I decided to lead 'Chieftain', a two-pitch VS on the main face at Fairhead. It was a climb that Calvin had put up the previous December, and I had already seconded it. But leading was always different. The start seemed steep and committing, and there was an awful lot of rock towering up above, but I managed it and the rest of the climb was no problem.

'Nice wee lead,' said Calvin when he got up to the ledge where I had belayed at the top of the first pitch. Ricky, a friend of Calvin's, was climbing with us that day. 'Nice wee lead,' said he as he too pulled up onto the ledge. Neither of them said 'for a girl', but it was hanging in the air. Just a bit further along the cliff Calvin and Sé had recently climbed 'Mannanán' and given it the grade of XS – Extremely Severe. There were a handful of other intimidating extremes scattered along the main face, including 'Equinox', 'Hurricane' and 'Doldrum', all the work of maverick climbing genius Paul McHugh.

I found it depressing that I would only ever be nibbling away at the edges of the cliff, picking off the VSs and the HVSs in the lower, less steep areas, but never having the strength to lead the big lines. Calvin agreed. Yes, he said, that's just the way things were, women simply didn't have the strength. So that was that then: I could never have the strength to tackle the big climbs that bristled at intervals along the cliff. They were for the men.

Calvin's family always treated me with great kindness and hospitality, and me being a wee Fenian didn't seem to matter. It was a bit different for my parents though. The Shankill Road was a foreign country in every way, and this man I was seeing (who was ten years older than me) was, or had been, married, and any details of separation or divorce didn't really lighten the burden of that. My parents worried, initially at least, that it would all end in tears, but very little was said. I stayed on at home – it was a lively and generally happy house and was very near my school – and I went away every weekend to meet up with Calvin.

I was still discovering wonders about him. He could make traps out of bits and pieces, light fires without matches and lasso rock spikes with ridiculous ease. One day he was leaning out over a mountain stream in Glenveagh, County Donegal, his ribbed green jumper soaking up the damp from the rushes. Concentrating on the peaty water, he dangled a bulrush with a worm wriggling in a slit at the end of it. I waited for him to catch a trout. 'Have you ever caught a fish like that?'

'No, but it was what you said – "The Song of Wandering Aengus" – I wanted to try it.' I had quoted the famous Yeats poem for him a few days earlier, and here he was checking to see if it might actually work.

I went out to the hazel wood,
Because a fire was in my head,
And cut and peeled a hazel wand,
And hooked a berry to a thread;
And when white moths were on the wing
And moth-like stars were flickering out,
I dropped the berry in a stream
And caught a little silver trout.

'But that was "hooked a *berry to a thread*",' I objected, but he just grinned and scrambled up.

It was getting late anyway. We'd been scouting all over the country for climbable but as yet unclimbed rock. The whole of Ireland was our domain, and after checking out sea cliffs in Cork and Kerry we'd moved on to Donegal. We both knew the Derryveagh Mountains well, but sharing them was a new pleasure. Whenever we got the map out I would tell Calvin the secrets of the place names – real secrets as he didn't even have the *cúpla focal*, the poor grasp of the language that most Irish people pick up at school. He did have one phrase, which was, ironically, from his time in the British Army: *Fág an bealach* (Clear the way) was the motto of the Royal Irish Fusiliers.

We had the great valley to ourselves, apart from a small herd of red deer. Calvin showed me the climbs at the back of the Poisoned Glen, the long meandering routes that ran up the great granite buttresses from one vegetated ledge to the next. Then he pointed out more direct lines – new, harder possibilities, as yet untouched – that we might climb together. We'd be back to lay claim to that precious rock in the spring.

We were booked into a B&B in the village of Ardara. I had been reading Doris Lessing, Simone de Beauvoir and Germaine Greer, but I was far from a brazen feminist as I signed in with a false name and wearing a ring from a Hallowe'en brack. The room the woman showed us up to overlooked the street. There were net curtains at the window and a vase of plastic flowers on the dressing table. We'd had a lot of great nights camping – it's hard to beat the blissful sanctuary of a small tent shared with your lover, especially if it's pouring rain outside – but this room was even more exciting. It was in the heart of conservative Ireland and under the very nose of the still-powerful church.

Chapter 8

Climbing was essential to Calvin, and his commitment to it was not negotiable. That was fine with me, as long as I was included in his plans, which I usually was. At the beginning of June 1975 he went to the Alps with English climber Lindsay Griffin. We were to meet up in Snell's Field when my school closed early in July. Lindsay was a very talented and ambitious young alpinist who had done many notable climbs in the Alps – both first ascents and first British ascents. He had been out of action for a year after having a toe amputated following severe frostbite, but now he was back and keener than ever. That summer he and Calvin made first British (and of course Irish) ascents of the North Face of Mont Blanc de Cheilon and the North Face of Mont Brûlé in the Swiss Alps, before bad weather drove them around to Chamonix.

Calvin got back to Snell's Field just in time for my twenty-third birthday. He brought me a present of an ice hammer. He looked half-Gypsy after his month in the mountains: lean and tanned and with a strip of red cloth twisted through his long dark hair to keep it out of his eyes. I was overjoyed to be with him again, and for a few days we made no climbing plans and thought only of each other.

Or at least I did – until one evening when he said he had to save his energy as he was heading off early the next day to do a route with Lindsay. What? Heading off climbing was one thing, but what was this business of saving his energy? Yes, he said, didn't I realise that was why most of the lads left their wives and girlfriends at home? No, I didn't know that. I was relatively new to all this after all, both the lovemaking and the alpinism. I thought it was much more likely that the wives and girlfriends hadn't wanted to spend their holidays in a grotty field where there was no toilet and no shower.

Calvin said that this thing about saving your strength was a well-established fact among athletes and soldiers, and that they had a saying in the army, 'Women weaken legs!' Oh they did, did they? Really? But I had to stop sulking and keep my jealousy to myself every time Lindsay swooped in when there was a good forecast and the two of them headed off to do a hard route. They were caught in a storm on one, and on another Calvin got frost-nip (mild frostbite), but they did succeed in climbing a new route on Mont Maudit, an outlier of Mont Blanc.

In the meantime I was determined to take responsibility for myself on some alpine climbs, and I teamed up with a couple of (male) Glenfoffany climbers for two rock routes in the pinnacles of the Aiguilles. There were some girls in the Glenfoffany Club, but none of them ever climbed enough to build up the experience necessary for the Alps, whereas I was now seen as a competent alpinist.

This was not a judgement I'd have made about myself, but in the five years since I'd started climbing I had done a great deal, and the ambitious young men in the club were more than happy to tie onto a rope with me. I did most of the leading on both of the climbs but we didn't get to the top of either of them as we had to turn back for fear of being benighted. On one we lost our way in a vertical maze of cracks and ledges, and on the other we were just too slow.

I learned a lot during that second season, but it was the scare I got on the Frendo Spur that made most of an impression on me. Alpine climbing, with its long demanding days on snow and rock, was many things, I discovered, but it was rarely simply fun. I'd seen the Frendo Spur from the air – from the startling vantage point of the cable car as it rose to the nearby summit of the Aiguille du Midi. The route had looked impressive but not too hard. There was 800 metres of rock to start with and then a narrowing ice ridge that ran up for another couple of hundred metres. In the black-and-white photograph in Gaston Rébuffat's *The Mont Blanc Massif: The Hundred Finest Routes* the ice arête looked good enough to eat. It curved up in an elegant white crest and I could even make out a line of little footprints running up it.

I had teamed up with Calvin's friend Ricky Cowan. We started climbing in the afternoon, and, as the rock section was relatively straightforward, we got to a reasonable bivouac ledge near the top of it before dark. This left us in a good position to tackle the ice early the next morning. It was best to get there while it was still well frozen from the night-time cold. The ridge of snow rose up at an encouragingly gentle angle, and we reckoned we'd be able to climb it and get the téléphérique down from the summit with time to spare before dark.

I tied my borrowed crampons onto my boots and double-checked them; I'd only worn them once before, on a winter trip to Scotland. We started up, moving in tandem, with Ricky in front and the rope strung out between us. It was very warm in spite of the snow and the altitude. Soon the ridge steepened and narrowed into a fin. There was a horrible downward swish to the snow slopes that dropped away on either side. We started pitching it: instead of climbing simultaneously, I stayed put while Ricky, the better and more experienced climber, climbed on ahead. When the rope was at full stretch, he stuck his ice axe into the snow and, slinging the rope around it for security, drew it in as I followed. Ever steeper and narrower, the little snow crest now gleamed with a slimy sheen and was much too soft. It was giving way to ice, but the ice was just a different variety of sugar. The climbing was not difficult, just terribly insecure, and I felt a rising tide of dread. 'We won't be able to get any proper belays, will we?' I asked Ricky.

'No.'

'Can we go back from here?'

'No. We'll just have to go on. And you know the score.'

Yes, I knew the score. If either of us slid off, the other probably wouldn't be able to hold the fall, with just an ice axe stuck in the collapsing snow as an anchor. We had ice screws with us, but they were designed for the lead climber to hammer into solid ice and clip their rope to as a runner before moving on up. They were useless in these conditions, and Ricky left his hanging on his harness.

We were heading for a bulge of rock below the horizontal summit ridge but it wasn't getting any closer. By now the early afternoon sun was at its hottest, and as we teetered up the steepening mush I was more frightened than I'd ever been. Ricky eventually got near enough to the rock to spot a peg that he thought he could reach. Small sheets of ice began to slither away under his crampons as he stretched to reach the peg. He leaned and stretched again, careful not to lose his balance, and managed to clip a karabiner through the eye of the peg. He quickly tied his rope to it to anchor himself, and I was able to let my breath out.

For hours now we had been dependent on ice axes pushed deep into the snow as anchor points while we belayed each other, and they were so fragile in the unstable conditions that instead of being a life-saving umbilical cord, the rope promised to drag both of us to our deaths if either of us slipped. But now Ricky was tied to the rock, the good solid rock, and as he pulled in the slack the rope became a reassuring link again. Which was just as well: as I climbed up the thin hem of ice that bordered the rock, it collapsed under me and he had to halt my slide.

Soon we were both secure and were beginning to think we'd make it, though we didn't dare put our double weight on the rusted peg. After being too hot all day and climbing in shirtsleeves, a cold mist swirled around us now, obliterating the summit ridge as well as the huge drops below. In spite of the cold it would take night-time temperatures to consolidate the finishing ice slopes so there was nothing for it but another bivy.

We scanned the rock but couldn't spot any ledges to stop at. We climbed higher and settled for a sloping stretch of rock and snow where there were a few old pegs in a crack. We tied into those and organised ourselves for the long wait – the sun was still high in the sky. Our boots were the only things we took off before getting into our sleeping bags, and we made sure they were securely tied to our belay. A dropped boot would mean disaster or, at the very least, the ignominy of having to shout or signal for a rescue.

We had a bivy tent with us – a light envelope of nylon – and when the temperature dipped we pulled it around us, and Ricky managed to cook a packet of savoury rice without letting anything fall. Once it got dark he went to sleep, but I kept slipping down and dangling uncomfortably in my harness. I manoeuvred out of the tiny shelter, still tied to the pegs and half inside my sleeping bag, and wedged myself between a couple of rocks, but I was freezing in no time and had to retreat to the cramped warmth. I jammed my ice axe into a patch of snow and spent the rest of the night hanging onto it. It was a long night, but we would live.

As the hours passed I had time to remember that this was a *Grande Course*, a big serious climb, and that when Calvin and Sé had done it the previous summer they'd also had to bivy a second time after they'd come upon a couple of young Spanish climbers who had lost their nerve. They'd organised a rescue for the young men and had waited with them until the rescue team lowered a cable from the ridge way above. I was beginning to see that the apprenticeship for alpinism was not something you could rush, unless you were very sure of yourself as a mountaineer. And I wasn't.

The other climbs that summer weren't nearly as fraught. Calvin and I did some good routes together, and then Bairbre arrived out in Chamonix and she and I went up to do the South Ridge of the Moine. I knew that repeating an alpine route was a bit of a cop-out, but I felt justified since I was taking full responsibility for her as well as myself. She had a cold and coughed all night as she lay in the open at the bivy, but she was still keen to go on in the morning. I led all the pitches confidently, knowing there would be no nasty surprises to stop me in my tracks, and Bairbre carried the rucksack.

'Come ON, Bairbre,' I shouted down as I gave the rope a tug. 'You'll have to hurry up!'

'I'll come in my own good time,' she yelled back.

And she did. But now I was the leader.

Chapter 9

Back in Ireland there was a new wave of climbers emerging in the South, and they, like Calvin and myself, were keen to put up new routes. We linked up with the most enthusiastic of them and formed our own club. We had our first official meeting at Fairhead in the autumn of 1976. I suggested we call the club Dal Riada – it was the name of the ancient Gaelic kingdom that took in north-east Antrim (around Fairhead) and part of western Scotland. The membership requirements were to be the same as those of the Spillikin Club: eight Very Severe leads to join and ten each year after that.

The backbone of the new club was Calvin and myself and three or four other strong adventurous partnerships. We were all Dublin-based as Calvin was now working in the city for a small company that made sleeping bags, and we shared cars to go climbing or exploring cliffs every weekend. Crossing the border into the North wasn't usually a problem, though the British soldiers at the checkpoints – teenagers with automatic rifles – would peer suspiciously into the car as soon as their torches showed that all the occupants, apart from me, were young males. One would ask for the boot to be opened, but the sight of the ropes and gear would immediately break the tension. 'Going climbing then, are you, mate?' the soldier would ask the driver. 'Done a bit of that myself.'

We criss-crossed the rest of the country too in search of unclimbed rock. The steep and promising limestone of the Ailladie sea cliff in the Burren was a recent discovery, and we had other limestone adventures on the escarpment of Tormore above Glencar Lake in Sligo. Usually we camped, but sometimes we'd share the weekend rent for a damp neglected cottage in a field full of rushes. Again and again we came back to Fairhead, to its huge stretches of untouched rock and the comparative luxury of our own hut.

Our most permanent hut was a tumbledown cottage at the Ballycastle end of the cliff. It was owned by the McBride family who had been farming there for seven generations. Séamus and his wife didn't mind if we used the cottage, the old family homestead, if we didn't mind the state of it, and they watched our comings and goings with bemused tolerance. If it was lashing outside we'd spend the day sitting around the smoky fire drinking tea. Books, climbing, books about climbing, education, philosophy, religion, films, music – the conversation never flagged and continued down in Hunter's pub, where it had to compete with the country and western songs on the jukebox.

Calvin ranged all over the crag and made it his own. He was catching up after his years in England. As well as climbing new routes, he did second ascents of the best of the existing climbs, 'freeing' the aid points as he went. We were often the only people on the cliff, with just the wild goats and peregrine falcons for company. 'I can't do it!' I'd howl up at him in rage, my cold skinned knuckles sliding out of the overhanging crack. 'It's too strenuous.'

'I'll give you a tight rope.'

I flailed up and scowled onto the belay ledge nursing my bloodied hands.

'Ah, come here to me love.'

Gradually I improved. I seconded Calvin on a lot of climbs, many of them first ascents of his, and sorting them into *doable* and *desperate* in my mind. The ones on the *doable* list were the ones I planned to lead – when I got up the nerve. I became stronger and found that hand-jamming was a good way of climbing steep cracks. I could slip my hand into a narrow slot and flex it against the coarse rock so that it wedged securely. Once it was well jammed I could hang from it comfortably without using up much energy, and then pull up easily with all the major muscles in my arm and shoulder contributing to the effort. Most other hand grips used smaller muscles and tendons in the hand and arm and were much more tiring. I could jam my fingers too, sometimes sliding them into thin cracks where other (male) climbers' fingers wouldn't fit. Even feet could be jammed into a crack and twisted sideways to be locked into place. This wasn't very comfortable, but it meant that you could climb up using just the inside of a narrow crack if there weren't any handholds on the outside. Jamming was a very useful technique on a cliff where almost every route had a crack in it.

I was in awe of Calvin's climbing – not just his strength and skill but the way he powered up steep lines like his very fine route 'Cúchulainn', a three-pitch groove-and-crack line that soared up a bulging wall. I had told him some of the old Irish myths and legends that I had loved as a child, and names like 'Cúchulainn' and 'Manannán' seemed to sit well with the impressive new routes he was putting up at Fairhead. He always climbed steadily and confidently, whether he was level with his meagre protection or well above it. He had the mental strength and physical confidence to presume he could do it, and just went ahead and did it.

At that time, doing first ascents – creating new routes – was the highest form of rock climbing you could engage in, and it wasn't long before I started putting up new climbs of my own. I edged up them cautiously and protected myself with care. I wanted to push myself, but just one step at a time. My new routes were in the VS and HVS grades. When I was attempting one of them, a handhold broke, and I fell and flipped upside down. I wasn't hurt, as I had the rope clipped to some protection in a crack and that held me well above the ground. Then, with the fear of falling out of the way, I felt a new confidence and climbed quickly back up to my high point and went on to finish the climb.

By the following year I was leading some of the Extremes, but I was still tentative – never sure that I could do something hard until

I had done it. When I was leading a crux at my limit – or at what I thought was my limit – I often hummed and hawed and stepped up and back down and up another bit until I was committed and couldn't retreat, while Calvin belayed me patiently from a ledge down below. I was more decisive when I was doing a first ascent; there was more to play for, and I didn't have a grade to distrust, a grade dreamed up by some strong-armed man.

On my first Extreme new route, I had to step up into a steep groove with no definite handhold. I was risking a sizeable fall if I slipped, as I was above my last protection. It was a gut-wrenching moment, but I did it, and didn't fall. When I woke the next morning in the hut and remembered what I'd done, I felt a wave of euphoria and gave myself the rest of the day off.

Whatever your grade, whatever your age, you're competing with yourself when you lead a hard climb. You judge the difficulty and the possible outcomes and then commit to the unknown. When you succeed you feel you've broken out of a chrysalis and now inhabit a better, braver, more powerful version of yourself. Testing your limits and surpassing your known self is at the heart of climbing.

But climbing is full of softer pleasures too – like that moment in an alpine dawn when you can switch off your head torch as the peaks all around you reveal themselves in the strengthening light. Or when you meet a friend at the top of the cliff, or in the pub, and he describes exactly how he did the crux moves of a particular climb, his hands moving excitedly in quick demonstration as he re-enacts those tense few seconds.

The fun, the exultation and the camaraderie that Calvin and I got from climbing far outweighed the harsh effort and discomfort that were often part of the game. And the fact that we shared it all made it more precious still. Our weekend world was an offshoot of the British mountaineering scene, but it had developed as a distinctly Irish all-island activity. We made occasional visits to Scotland for winter climbing, or to Wales to rock climb, but there was no traffic in the other direction, mainly because of the Troubles.

In North Wales, Calvin introduced me to the famous rock climbs

I'd read about in countless mountaineering books, but I found them disappointing – for quality and drama they didn't compare with the big routes at Fairhead. One aspect of the British climbing scene that we did appreciate was its climbing magazines, as we had nothing comparable at home. We got *Mountain* magazine, the magazine of record for the mountaineering world, and read about the latest notable ascents in the Alps and the Himalayas. Some British rock climbing was covered too, and there were stunning photographs of climbers on the sun-soaked walls of Yosemite Valley in California.

But there were no women. Well, there were girls, but only in the ads. They appeared wrapped in their boyfriends' oversize duvet jackets, looking petite and feminine, and nude, or emerging coyly from the latest expedition sleeping bags, bags that were obviously not their own. Naked girls were common in climbing gear ads. Berghaus had one lassie who was viewed from behind wearing nothing but their new lightweight rucksack frame, and Javlin advertised their latest men's fleece jacket by draping it seductively around an alluring female who wore nothing else. The best known ad was for Edelrid ropes. The German rope manufacturer chose to feature a naked girl with a rope coiled around her up to her shoulders and promised that it would be uncoiled gradually over a series of ads in forthcoming issues.

Women's place was clearly marked in the lads' mag *Crags* as well, another English publication that first appeared in the mid 1970s. Sexism seemed to be one of the mainstays of its editorial policy, going by the crudeness of the ads. I paid no attention to the girly pictures, not consciously anyway, as attractive female faces and bodies were used to advertise all sorts of things at the time. These images were part of the 'pretty girlfriend' world which I knew must have its own rules and which I knew nothing about. It was as unreal and irrelevant to me as a James Bond film.

I did wonder if people considered my mountaineering to be unfeminine, as I was so willing to rough up my hands and wear shapeless clothes – the outdoor brands hadn't started designing for women yet – but I was too happy and comfortable in the climbing scene to give more than a passing thought to that.

Right through the 1970s, neither *Mountain* nor *Crags* had any pictures of women climbing, and you'd never have guessed, from the content of either magazine, that a woman, Jo Scarr, had led 'Cenotaph Corner' in Wales, for years the hardest climb in Britain, and that she had led it as far back as 1960. Finally, in 1980, there was a photograph of American climber Coral Bowman in *Mountain*. She was climbing steep rock, and this was the first public acknowledgement that hard climbing was a game for women too – the first that I spotted at any rate.

I didn't experience any sexism from Irish climbers, having only ever had support from the people I climbed with. I always compared myself to the men in our club – the strongest climbers in the country – and was disappointed when I usually fell short. I was leading Extreme climbs regularly now and wasn't aware that there were few enough women in Britain climbing at the same level.

For a long time there were no other women in Dal Riada. It would have been a great boost to me to see another girl strapping on her helmet and uncoiling her ropes to lead a hard climb at Fairhead or at the Burren sea cliff. Competition would have trumped my natural caution and motivated me to try harder climbs. But from the time I started to challenge myself at Fairhead I had to wait nearly another decade for that.

Chapter 10

'How'd you like to go on an expedition to the Himalayas?' asked Calvin one Friday evening in the spring of 1976. He had come to meet me at the train station in Belfast, and we were queuing to see *The Return of the Pink Panther* at a nearby cinema. His eyes were alight with excitement.

The plan was to organise an expedition for the summer of 1977 to tackle unclimbed peaks in the Indian Himalaya, but there was a plan for the coming summer too, in just a few months' time. Calvin wanted to go on a reconnaissance trip to the same area, with Sé, Valerie and myself – if we wanted to come.

Of course we wanted to come!

Calvin chuckled his way through the film, but I was in too much of a whirl to take any of it in. My first thought was my long hair; I'd have to get it cut because I'd be going for weeks without washing it. And the dates: would I have to give up work? What would my parents say about such a trip? And then there was 'the pill'. I'd have to go back to the Family Planning clinic for advice because the contraceptive pill could cause problems at altitude.

You couldn't buy contraceptives in Ireland in the 1970s, and no one I knew was actually on the pill, but there was this one place, a clinic in Synge Street in Dublin, where you could get them – even as a single girl. I had called in there earlier in the year – you didn't even need an appointment – and was relieved to find that the doctors and nurses who staffed the place were reassuringly pleasant and professional. They didn't need to know anything about what I was up to or with whom, and were only concerned about things like blood pressure. The law forbidding the sale of contraceptives was sidestepped by there being no charge, just a voluntary donation. Priceless!

But now I'd have to go back for advice because the pill was 'contraindicated at altitude', or so I'd read in a climbing magazine in an article about women going trekking in the Himalayas. There were no articles about women going *climbing* in the Himalayas. As it happened the clinic doctor had never heard about the link between the pill and the retention of fluid that can cause pulmonary oedema, a form of altitude sickness, but she was able to advise me anyway.

I didn't have to give up work because we were able to fit our trip into the summer holidays, and, as for my parents, they didn't express any strong views for or against my holiday plans. They must have been worried – we were going away as two couples, and we were going to climb in the Himalayas – but I was now living in a flat with Sheila and gave no thought to their concerns.

We were travelling to the Kishtwar area of Kashmir in north-western India. Kashmir! The romance of it! There had been some exploratory expeditions to Kishtwar – European and Japanese – but very few of the peaks had been climbed. The bus from Delhi was hot and crowded, and the smells were overwhelming. It was a two-day journey north, and we weren't long into it when I was horrified to realise that I had diarrhoea.

Each time the bus stopped, men would head off to one side of the road to go to the toilet, and women to the other. When Valerie and I followed the women, we were dismayed to find that the facilities were just a concrete yard with a lot of small holes in it. The Indian women could squat in the privacy of their saris, but Valerie and I were without a shred of decency in our shorts. All we could do was take turns and stand in front of each other to show that we weren't total barbarians.

It was a great relief to get to Kishtwar, the town at the end of the road, cool on its high grassy plain. It wasn't on any tourist trail, and the only accommodation was a dak bungalow – a guest house used mainly by government officials. There was just one room available, with two double beds, but it had its own shower and toilet. After the days on the bus it was sheer luxury.

The following day, still in shorts and T-shirts, we headed to the local bazaar to buy food for our five weeks in the mountains. The narrow laneways and tiny stalls looked medieval, and the food on sale was all dried and stored loose in huge sacks. We had hoped to buy packets and tins, but when we left the market we were weighed down with bags of flour, rice, potatoes, lentils and peas – food that was heavy to transport but low in calories – as well as a few jars of jam and honey. All four of us lost a lot of weight on that trip.

Back at the guest house, we had just laid all the food out in the shade of the veranda when a policeman appeared. He demanded to see our passports and other official documents and interrogated Calvin and Sé. Then he suddenly turned to Valerie and me. 'Are you married?' We said no, smiling at such a personal question. 'Are you virgin?' Self-preservation prompted us both to say yes, in unison.

We were totally ignorant of the local religious and cultural sensitivities, which, as it happened, were predominantly Muslim, not that that would have meant much to us at the time. Sé told us later that he'd been approached by some local youths who offered to pay him to leave the curtains of our room open at night so they could watch any action. Valerie and I, two recently qualified primary-school teachers, thought of ourselves as anything but wild and were shocked that we should be such a source of scandal.

The four of us had a very memorable summer in the Himalayas. Sé and Calvin attempted two unclimbed peaks, but avalanches and the unsuitable food stopped them getting far on either.

Sé never made it onto the expedition proper. He died the following spring, killed by a fall at Fairhead. He and Valerie were the only people at the cliff that day. He fell when his abseil anchor failed, and Valerie had to leave him lying injured in the rough grass and brambles at the foot of the cliff while she ran for help, scrambling up the gully and racing over the boggy ground to the McBrides' farmhouse.

I couldn't come close to imagining what she must have gone through: the shock, the fear, the sliver of hope. Sé died in the helicopter on the way to hospital in Belfast. He was just thirty. St Agnes's Church in Crumlin was filled to overflowing for his funeral. He had been a friend of both Calvin's and mine, and we missed him.

Sé's death was my first experience of losing someone close to me, and it filled me with fear at the frailty of life. This wasn't related to climbing. Sé's fall had been an accident in the same way that a road crash was an accident, and it didn't affect our climbing. What I struggled with was the reality of Valerie's situation. I couldn't bear to accept how fragile life was and how easily I could be in her shoes, having lost the love of my life.

Her grief tunnelled a hole in me, and I, fair-weather friend that I discovered myself to be, turned away to protect myself and then busily patched the hole with the crowded days of my own sunny life. Over the next few years Valerie gradually stopped climbing, and we met up less and less often before eventually drifting out of contact.

Chapter 11

When Calvin and I went back to Kishtwar the following year, in 1977, it was as members of a properly constituted expedition. As with most expeditions at the time, the 'team' was an informal grouping of like-minded friends and acquaintances. Calvin was the leader, for bureaucratic purposes, but all the decision-making was done democratically. We had the official blessing of the FMCI and with that came a grant. We also received a grant from the London-based Mount Everest Foundation, a charity that supports mountain exploration, and we got sponsorship, in cash or in kind (food, medical supplies and climbing equipment) from various Irish businesses. We got generous donations too from climbing clubs and individual climbers, all of which helped to defray our costs.

The previous year, on our way back from the mountains, we had been pinned down in Kishtwar for days by the monsoon rains. It was decided that this year's trip should begin earlier: at the start of June. This was a full month before the end of the school year, and I was thinking of giving up my job when, to my surprise, my father suggested another solution.

With the build-up to the expedition he was seeing our climbing in a new light. We had got grants and sponsorship, and Joss Lynam was going with us. Joss was the well-respected public face of Irish mountaineering, and my father had read articles of his in the *Irish Times*. My father realised too that we, but particularly Calvin, were recognised as serious mountaineers and that we were supported by the national body – the FMCI.

He encouraged me to apply for leave of absence on the same terms as a teacher on a national amateur team might. I'd never heard of leave of absence before and didn't think it likely that the Department of Education would see a mountaineering expedition as comparable to, say, the GAA All-Stars team that went to America every year, especially as I was a woman, but it was worth a try. Joss wrote a letter to support my application, and I was granted unpaid leave for the last month of the school term.

On our reconnaissance the previous year, Calvin and Sé had picked out two unclimbed peaks as worthwhile objectives, and now we had climbing permits from the Indian Mountaineering Federation to attempt them. Himalayan climbing permits serve various purposes for the host country. They are a source of revenue, and they enable the authorities to keep track of what has and hasn't been climbed and by how many. Most important of all, they help regulate the movement of foreigners and others in border areas. India, Pakistan, Afghanistan, China, Bhutan and Nepal all share the Himalayas, and all have borders running along particular peaks and ridges. Some of them have internal fault lines too, often in mountainous areas where historic or ethnic tensions flare up periodically.

It is customary to allocate an army liaison officer to each expedition and he fills the dual role of government representative and general facilitator for the visitors. Our man, Captain I. P. Singh of the Regiment of Artillery of the Indian Army, was waiting for us at the airport in Delhi. He was a young and dapper Sikh officer whose turban never had a crease awry. We found him to be unfailingly polite, hard-working and good-humoured, but, initially at least, he wasn't sure what to make of us.

Joss had been born in London and had served as an engineer (and officer) with the British Army in India from where he had organised his first Himalayan expedition in 1946. With his residual British accent he clearly belonged to the officer and gentleman class that had characterised the previous generation of Himalayan climbers.

The rest of us clearly did not. There was Emmett Goulding, a house painter, who was an experienced and highly regarded alpinist; Anthony Latham, a strong climber who, as a twenty-two-year-old medical student, was filling the role of expedition doctor; and there was Calvin, who had none of the formality or self-importance of a traditional leader. And finally there was me, a female.

I.P.'s first and most acute problem was how to address us. He always spoke to Calvin as 'Torrans', intoned in a loud and emphatic way to show due respect to the expedition leader. He had no difficulty using Emmett's or Anthony's first names, but he baulked at calling Joss by his because Joss was twice his age. He never got used to me being around at all. Himalayan expeditions were still a male preserve, and for days he avoided addressing me until he finally settled on 'Lady Clare'.

Our food supplies were much better than on the previous trip as we had some dried food from home and were able to buy tinned food in Delhi. Anthony, Emmett, Calvin and I organised the food and equipment into loads while Joss and I.P. negotiated with a small group of men for their services as porters. Once again we stayed in the dak bungalow at Kishtwar. As before, the walk-in took us six days, and it was only on the last day that our small cavalcade of sahibs and porters got their first view of the mountains.

We came out of a rocky river gorge onto a rolling plain and saw the beautiful shapes of the high mountains stand out against the dark-blue sky. This was where we'd site our base camp. But we still had a wide river to cross to get there. The river hadn't been a problem the previous year as we'd been able to cross at a narrow point where a slide of avalanche debris had bridged it, but now we were going to need help. According to I.P., this should be available from some nomads who had an encampment further up the valley.

As we made our way along the plain towards a clump of thatched stone huts, people of all ages began to appear and converge on us. These were the Bakarwal, the nomads who herded big flocks of sheep and goats in the high valleys each summer. They were tall and strikingly handsome, and I.P. told us that they claimed to be descended from

Alexander the Great. The men had dark beards and colourful turbans, and the women wore elaborate silver jewellery and kept their long black hair braided and coiled under little embroidered caps.

Two of the men came to meet us, and Joss and I.P. began negotiating a price for transporting us and our gear across the river on horseback. It had started to snow as the porters were being paid off, and a small wiry woman, the matriarch of the extended family, insisted on bringing me into one of the huts to sit by the fire. The woman's name was Bachot, according to I.P., and she could have been aged anything from forty to seventy-five.

She took my cold hands in hers to warm them up and as we sat in the dim smoky light, she talked non-stop to her three daughters while never taking her eyes off me. She had probably never seen a European woman at close quarters before, and I was glad I'd changed out of my shorts and into long trousers earlier in the day. I didn't fancy having my pale freckled knees laid bare to so many interested female eyes.

The young women were shy and moved gracefully in their long flowing robes as they fed babies, prepared food and went outside to manage the horses. Later, they served us rice and bowls of tea with lumps of goat's butter in it. And then the questions started. They were all directed at me, with I.P. as translator. Which one was I married to? My answer – Calvin - was a white lie, of course. Was I Joss's daughter? (Joss was in his early fifties by then.) How many children did I have? They were amazed, dismayed even, that I was twenty-four but still had no children.

Before we left, Bachot conducted a little ceremony. She brought me outside, and when everyone had filed out behind us, she put her cap on my head, drew her shawl around me and insisted that I slip on a heavy silver bangle that one of her daughters had been wearing. Then she declared me to be her sister.

OK, but what do I do now? What should I give her? I shot a questioning glance at Joss and I.P., but they both looked blank. I could see that she was interested in my thick red mountaineering socks, but I needed those. Then I thought of the silver chain that Bairbre had given me before I left home. It had a dog tag on it with my name, date of birth and blood group. (What did Bairbre think was going to befall me?) Bachot was happy to accept the chain, and we said goodbye. I wondered what she made of us, a travelling group like her own but for the pointless purpose of climbing unclimbed mountains. At least she didn't see me as a source of scandal.

Base camp, at 3,800 metres, would be our home for the next five weeks. We pitched our three small tents on a stretch of level sandy grass near a clear stream and unpacked our supplies. There were gentians, bog cotton and edelweiss scattered through the grass and little yellow and purple flowers that Joss identified as rock roses and mountain primroses. It was a lovely place, and the more time we spent in the harsh mineral world of rock, ice and snow higher up, the more we appreciated those little flowers on our return.

We were away from base camp for days at a time, carrying loads, doing reconnaissance, setting up high camps, and, of course, climbing. I.P. stayed in base camp but was always on the lookout for our return, scanning the high moraine ridge for the first exhausted figure to appear. He made excellent chapatis (flat breads) on the open fire and would have them ready and still warm for us when we got back. One evening he made a terrific curry but was very coy about it. Only after I'd gone to bed did he reveal that it was made from goats' testicles brought by the nomads.

Base camp was the haven where we could wash and put on clean clothes and rest and read. Calvin and I shared a little tent whose cramped dimensions were soothing after the big-sky exposure of days in the mountains. And our sleeping bags zipped together very neatly.

Life above base camp was much more streamlined. The only items we brought with us were the essentials for climbing, eating and shelter. If we were carrying gear up the glacier to establish a high camp, we brought tents and supplies of food for a number of days, and our pack-frame rucksacks bulged so high behind our heads that they got in the way when we looked up at the sky. When we were packing our sacks for climbing we were more ruthless: each extra kilo would take its toll as we kicked our crampons into steep snow slopes and pulled breathlessly onto little rock ledges.

Our food supplies were minimal and light. We stuffed Alpen, chocolate and packs of Erin dried soup and stew in around the bivouac gear in our sacks, along with little bags of instant coffee, tea and powdered milk. One thing we didn't carry was toiletries, and I was glad, as I always was in the mountains, to be far from ordinary life with its need for deodorants and mirrors. Our water was limited as it had to be melted from snow using our precious paraffin supply, but it was interesting to find that the fifth day (and night) in the same sweaty clothes without a wash, was no worse than the third.

On our very first carry, when we got to the crest of the moraine we looked out over the Sarbal glacier to a spectacular line-up of unclimbed peaks. We had permits to attempt two of them and stood for a while like emperors surveying the possibilities. At this distance everything looked climbable. We couldn't see the impassable icy overhangs or hear the slither of avalanches.

The first peak we attempted had been spotted years before by members of a German expedition, and they, with an unforgivable lack of imagination, had named it Eiger. We walked a long way up the glacier to establish an advanced base camp near the foot of it, and it was on one of our hard days of shuttling gear and food to its base that I fell into the crevasse. After being rescued by Emmett, he and Joss and I roped up to walk out on the glacier proper. It took us a couple of hours to catch up with Calvin and Anthony, and then I had the chance to defuse some of the horror of the fall by retelling all the details.

After three days of ferrying loads, we set up camp at the foot of Eiger but soon realised we would be wasting our time attempting it: there were regular avalanches blasting down all the feasible routes. So it was back to base camp for a rest. Anthony, the medical student, had been the fittest and strongest of us on all the carries despite having a persistent toothache, but by the time we got back to base camp he was almost unrecognisable, his face badly swollen by an abscess. With great steadiness and courage, and the aid of a small mirror, he operated on the throbbing tooth and drained the abscess. The following day, two of the Bakarwal rode across the river with a spare horse and asked him to ride down the valley with them to see a woman who was very ill. He did so, and diagnosed a serious heart problem, one that was well beyond his expertise to treat.

We set up a camp at the base of our second objective and studied it. It had an English name: Cathedral Peak, and was just under 5,400 metres. These mountains weren't very high by Himalayan standards, but they were technically difficult. Looking from the glacier, it was impossible to judge just how difficult. It looked as if the best route would be up a big snow slope and then onto some steepening rock that led to the summit ridge. We hoped to do it in two days.

We started up at 3 a.m., when the snow was well frozen, and made good progress crunching up it in our crampons. It was afternoon by the time we got to where the snow slope, now soft and unreliable, ran up against the rock. It looked like a good place to stop for the night as we could level out a sleeping space and get a solid anchor from the rock above.

At the edge of the slope there was a big drop with a cornice – a meringue of soft snow – curling out over the top of it. We started to dig out the cornice with our ice axes, and after a lot of effort we had fashioned a sofa-sized hollow for Joss, Emmett and Anthony to sit in for the night and, just below it, a big armchair scoop for Calvin and myself. Because of the precariousness of our perch, with the snow slope below us on one side and a huge drop on the other, we had to stay tied in at all times. We were all within arm's reach of each other, closely linked in a short web of ropes that ran from our harnesses to the belay anchor.

But I had a problem: how was I going to manage to go to the toilet? Toilet issues loom large for all women who are active in the outdoors, but this situation had unique difficulties. It had been twelve hours since I'd buckled on my harness, and we'd been climbing continuously all day, with just a short break for a drink and a Marathon bar. Now I'd have to take my harness off and tie a loop of rope around my waist for security, with a few metres of slack to get me to the edge of the drop, and then ask everyone to politely look the other way. And now, of all times, my period had started. Thank goodness for tampons, I thought, patting the pocket of my knee breeches. Yes, I'd remembered.

It was still broad daylight when we settled down for the night. Our boots and crampons were the only things we took off, and our web of rope now reached down into each of the five sleeping bags as we had to stay attached to the belay. The snow seat was comfortable, snug even, in spite of the drop to the shadowy couloirs hundreds of metres below our feet. A goodnight kiss, and I slept for ten hours straight. At 6 a.m., we got moving. The plan was to leave our bivy gear and climb on up to the summit. Then, with a bit of luck, we'd make it back down to the bivouac before dark.

We had a few hundred metres to climb to reach a big ridge and then we would follow that to the top. It would be all rock now. Calvin led off first, and it was soon obvious that the climbing was quite hard. Anthony followed, and I was getting ready to start up when Joss said, out of the blue, that we three (Emmett, himself and myself) should wait at the bivy and leave it to Calvin and Anthony, the two strongest climbers, to go for the summit on their own.

Hang on! Where had that come from? When had that been discussed? Emmett didn't say anything, so he must be in agreement. Joss said he felt 'baggagey' (a burden) and that we'd just slow the others down. Huh! Joss could speak for himself. I felt strong and fit and wasn't going to turn back now, at eight o'clock in the morning on a day of perfect weather when there was only some rock between me and the summit of a hitherto unclimbed Himalayan peak.

I shouted up to Calvin that the others were staying put. 'OK,' came the reply, 'Come on.' Relieved, I rushed to get to grips with the rock. The climbing was steep and strenuous and the rock loose in places. Calvin and Anthony shared the leads on the rope lengths up to the ridge, and I followed, carrying the rucksack. My other task was to take out all the protection pegs they'd hammered in. It was hard slow work at that altitude, and as I banged away with my peg hammer I wondered if I should have stayed below.

The ridge leading towards the summit was more difficult than it had looked from the bivy, and we soon found our way blocked by a big buttress of rock. There was only one weakness in it: a wet bulging crack with ice at the back. The summit was just a couple of hundred metres away, almost within reach, but this nasty overhanging thing would be a struggle to climb even at sea level and it stopped us dead. We hadn't expected this. According to our altimeter, we were already at 5,400 metres – higher than the 5,370 metres given for the summit. The map must be wrong. It was just a simple sketch map which Joss had got from a Japanese expedition that had reconnoitred the area a few years earlier.

Details of mountaineering expeditions were published in the yearly journals of national alpine associations, and Joss had an impressive library of them in the attic of his house in Dublin. He had researched the climbing history of the Kishtwar Himalaya, and, at his request, the leader of the Japanese expedition had posted on a copy of his hand-drawn map. When we'd first seen the map laid out on the gleaming wood of Joss's dining-room table, a white sheet of paper with spidery black lines to represent the mountain ridges and little triangles to denote the summits, the big blank spaces in between had glowed with adventure and promise. But now we had come to a full stop. We sorted out the ropes to begin abseiling. Cathedral Peak would remain unclimbed for many years to come.

Back with Emmett and Joss at the bivouac, we rested and waited for the snow slopes below us to freeze. During the night there were signs that a storm was building, and soon lightning was flashing continuously in the distance. This was a big worry as our planned descent was down a long snow gully that would be raked by avalanches if a storm broke. At first light we started abseiling, but by late morning we had to take refuge on a rocky shoulder. The storm hadn't materialised, but it was just too warm, and avalanches of soft snow had started sliding down the runnels on each side of our island of rock. Again we'd have to sit it out until the cool of darkness. The sun beat down, glaring off the sea of snow. We hid behind sun cream and dark goggles and we melted snow for tea and instant soup, too dehydrated to care that we'd run out of food.

When the sun went down it began to get cold – cold enough to consolidate the snow a bit and to make us put on all our spare clothes.

We started moving when it was fully dark, warming up in minutes as we ploughed down the soft slopes.

Soon I found I couldn't see properly. My sweaty hair was coming into my eyes, pressed tight by my balaclava and helmet, and my glasses and goggles were steamed up. What was I doing still wearing my goggles – in the dark? I had four layers of clothes on when we started down, but the physical effort and tension of descending the steep snow soon made me overheat. I was reduced to an incompetent mess in no time, but there never seemed to be a good place to stop to take anything off.

Lower down the slope the angle eased, and the other three put their rope away and continued descending steadily in the moonlight. They strode down quickly, converting skids into long strides and using their ice axes to brake anytime they started to slide out of control. Kicking your cramponned heels in to steady yourself at each step gives some security, but when the snow clogs up the teeth of your crampons it feels like you're skating on plastic bags. If you were unroped on this terrain and took off on an icy patch you'd go a long way.

I insisted on keeping the rope on and descended facing in to the slope, kicking in step after step, while Calvin belayed me from above. It was secure but slow. How were the others so confident on this shitty snow? Was it because they hadn't spent a day in fear on disintegrating snow on the Frendo Spur? An hour or two later we could see the three head torches bobbing around together way below. They must be down on the glacier and back at the tents already.

Calvin's patience was at its limit by the time we got to the bottom of the slope. I was exhausted and completely demoralised, and now there was a small river running along the ice where there hadn't been one before. I jumped it, knowing I'd slip – and I did, but we were still roped and Calvin pulled me out. That was the last straw, and I gave in to tears. In the warmth of Calvin's concern I pulled myself together, and we walked on, his arm around me, our head torches picking out the crampon marks that the others had left in the ice.

I felt terrible. I'd been very slow on the descent, and while that wouldn't have mattered if it had just been Calvin and me, I felt I'd let myself down in front of the others. They'd have guessed that I was overcautious because I was fearful. And they weren't. Maybe women weren't tough enough for expeditions after all.

By now our time was running out, and when Emmett and I.P. left to organise the porters, a plan was hatched for one last climb: an attempt on an unclimbed 5,000-metre peak above base camp. I didn't think it looked very attractive and volunteered to stay to mind our tents. A few youngsters from a different nomad group had started pilfering things, including my red socks, and someone had to stay to safeguard the camp.

The ascent went well and took just two days. Calvin, Anthony and Joss gained ground easily on the lower part of the mountain and, after bivouacking, climbed some good rock pitches to the summit. Joss took the trouble to name the peak in Urdu, the local language. He called it Khel Parbat – Ibex Peak – as they had seen one of the wild mountain goats up there. He said that it was the first Himalayan mountain ever to be climbed by a completely Irish team. Moreover, it was a first ascent. And if anyone would know that for a fact, Joss would.

Well, I'd missed out on that one.

With all our bags packed, we waited on the riverbank for the nomads and their horses. The river was wilder now. Summer meltwater from the glaciers had made it deeper and faster, and it rushed through the plain, trapping gravelly islands between its multiple branches. The day wore on, and when there was still no sign of the nomads, we started to transport the bags across ourselves. We each had three heavy bags to carry, and this meant crossing every stretch of river five times. The freezing water felt as if it was stripping the skin from our sunburnt legs.

Each section was deeper than the last, and it was early afternoon by the time we had all the bags piled up on an island that was roughly halfway across. The next section looked wide and wild. We each shouldered a big rucksack and formed a circle with our arms over each other's shoulders before stepping slowly into its rush. I soon felt the powerful current almost lift me off my feet. 'It's too strong,' I shouted over the noise of the racing water. 'We're not going to make it!'

'Shut up! Stop that!' yelled Calvin. I was so surprised – he never spoke like that – that I shut up and pressed on.

But our circle faltered anyway, and a moment later I was swept away. I went hurtling downriver, face in the freezing water, immobilised by the heavy pack frame on my back. Then the current flipped me over, and as I surfaced the water broke up into droplets on my sunglasses. A scene from the film *The Missouri Breaks* flashed through my mind, the part where the water drips and splashes on the camera lens as it films the guy drowning.

I kicked down and tried hard to get some purchase on the riverbed, but it was a turmoil of moving stones. I was powerless, and I had time to be scared. With my face just above water, I screamed 'CALVIN!' and heard Anthony shouting to me not to worry as he and Calvin raced along the bank. Then Calvin jumped back in and managed to grab hold of my pack frame and pull me to shore.

There were cuts and bruises all over my legs, but otherwise I was in one piece. Soon I had dry clothes on and was warming up in a sleeping bag while Anthony kept an eye on me for signs of shock or hypothermia. Being the damsel in distress didn't appeal to me at all, especially after having been so slow coming down off Cathedral Peak, and I decided I was fine as soon as I stopped shivering. Going on wasn't an option because of the high level of the river, and we had no choice but to stay put on our island. The water level would be lower in the morning after the night-time freeze.

The others had just started to pitch the tents when the Bakarwal appeared in the distance. They were five: Bachot's eldest son, Nur Allam, plus his two brothers and two brothers-in-law. They crossed the river to our island but then rode away to the far tip of it. What were they at? They wheeled around and then came galloping madly towards us, a whirlwind of warriors with the tails of their turbans flying out behind them. As they came closer, we saw that they were waving big sticks, and we waited nervously while they bore down on us. But they were only showing off. They reined in their horses at the last minute and were all smiles as they leaned down to shake hands.

They told us that the woman with the heart condition, whom Anthony had visited, had died, and they had been down to her funeral, but now, they said, they would sort everything out. They asked our men to take off their duvet jackets as the bright colours would frighten the horses, and passed them their own brown jackets instead. They insisted on taking Joss across first – 'Buddha,' they called him. Clearly age beat damsels hands down.

When it was my turn, I clamped my knees to the woollen blanket on the horse's back and sat rigid with fear as one of the Bakarwal calmly led it through the strong current. The water came right up to the man's chest at the deepest point. 'Jaysus!' was all I could say to Joss when I wobbled over to sit beside him on the gravel.

In the Poisoned Glen, County Donegal, where we explored the big granite cliffs.

Calvin climbing in the Mournes in 1966.

The first Fairhead climbing meet in 1967. From left: Paul McDermott, Jimmy Heffernan, Tony Ingram, Paul McHugh, Paddy O'Leary, Calvin Torrans, Bruce Rodgers.

Photo with kind permission of the Goulding family.

Below: With Calvin near our base camp, Irish Kishtwar Expedition, 1977.

On the Sarbal Glacier, Kishtwar.

Nur Allam with his child. He was one of the nomads who rescued us when our river crossing went badly wrong.

Photo with kind permission of the Goulding family.

Calvin and English climber Nipper Harrison on a bivouac ledge during their ascent of the Nose – the famous multi-pitch 'big wall' climb on El Capitan, Yosemite Valley.

Photo: Graham Everitt.

A Dal Riada hut group at Fairhead in 1983. From bottom left: Calvin Torrans, Keefe Murphy, me, Ian Rea, Tom Ryan (with arms folded), unknown, Eddie Cooper, unknown, Andy Dawe, Phil Holmes, Dawson Stelfox (seated).

Photo with kind permission of the Goulding family.

Chapter 12

Back in the late 1970s, it was relatively easy to buy a house in Ireland, if you had a steady salary coming in. Our house was in a new estate in the north Wicklow town of Bray, about 10 kilometres from where my parents lived. It was convenient enough for both our workplaces as Calvin was working as a mountaineering instructor in the Tiglin Adventure Centre further south in County Wicklow.

I was at home on my own the day the Franciscan called. I had heard in passing that the new Catholic parish on our side of Bray was to be run by members of the Franciscan order rather than by the usual couple of priests, but what was bringing him to our house? Outside of my school duties I only ever went inside a church for funerals.

The Franciscan seemed to fill all the space at the door. In his brown monk's robe and bare sandaled feet, he was a medieval apparition in the half-finished housing estate.

'And a very good day to you, Mrs . . . ?'

'Oh . . . , hello, ah . . . O'Brien.' I didn't dare give my real name. As a non-churchgoing teacher, I couldn't risk coming to the attention of any clerics. It might cost me my job.

'Well, it's very nice to meet you, Mrs O'Brien.' He held out his hand. 'We're going around getting to know everyone in the new parish. There's so many new houses here now. And you'll have seen where the new church is being built?' I nodded. 'But the temporary place we're using is still going strong, and I'd like to give you the times of the Masses. And we'll be having a get-together there next week, for all the new parishioners.'

'Ah no' – should I call him 'Father' or 'Brother'? – 'that's all right, no we're not . . . mm, we're not . . . Catholics.'

'Oh, are you not?' He was still smiling.

Fear flooded me, and I couldn't think straight. I was sure he knew everything. He knew my name, and that I was a Catholic, a Catholic living with a divorced man. And that I was teaching in a neighbouring parish – he surely knew that too. Had the parish priest, the school manager, given him my address? They must be checking up on me.

As a teacher in a parish school I was responsible for passing on the Catholic faith to the children in my class. I even prepared them for their First Holy Communion and Confirmation, depending on what class I was allocated, and I stood with them and smiled for the camera when their parents took photographs on their special day. I had no choice. All of the state's 'national' schools were church-run parish schools. And now the priests must be checking my fitness to teach in their schools. They'd want to know who else was in the house and whether I went to Mass regularly.

Two thoughts scattered all others: I'd lose my job, and my father, who was now the Chief Inspector for Primary Schools, would be disgraced.

'I'll leave you some parish literature anyway,' he said. He must know.

'Oh no, thanks very much but that's all right. Bye now,' I said. I felt sick. I went to close the door, but he put his foot in it. He put his big bare foot in its black leather sandal onto the new carpet in our hall, and I couldn't close the door. He was still smiling, daring me to close it. I couldn't let him in another inch or he'd find out everything. He might spot a letter addressed to Calvin on the kitchen table or see a pair of underpants on the clothes line out the back. And then I'd be finished.

I gave the door a little push, and he stepped back. His smile was sad now as he gave me a last look. 'I'll say goodbye so, Mrs O'Brien.'

I closed the door.

Oh God, how could I put up with that? Afraid to open my own front door? We'd have to go away. We'd have to get married.

When Calvin came home, he said I shouldn't worry, that there wouldn't be any trouble. But how would he know? He hadn't grown up in the shadow of an all-powerful church. He said we should go away anyway, to climb, and if we could get married while we were away, then all the better.

Neither of us put any value on getting married. It was just an annoying bit of bureaucracy that had no relevance to our commitment to each other. And who'd want to be a *wife* anyway? As a married woman, *a little wifey*, you'd be a second-class citizen, just an add-on to your husband. My mother sometimes got letters addressed to 'Mrs Michael Sheridan'. And as for *housewife*, I'd seen how she had filled that role for almost thirty years. Her labour – housekeeping and bearing and rearing children – was unceasing and unpaid, and we all took her completely for granted. Well, that wasn't going to be me.

Months went by after that without any further parish visits, and my fear of the Franciscan subsided. My parents and Calvin were on friendly terms whenever they happened to meet, but there was always an underlying awkwardness as my mother was anxious to keep up the pretence that Calvin and I weren't living together. I didn't mention anything about marriage to them, but I knew they'd be happier if our situation were formalised. And the only way to do that was to get married, and that meant going abroad.

Divorce was still illegal in Ireland, and Calvin and Marsha's divorce wouldn't be recognised. We decided we would go away in a year or two but in the meantime we had another big trip planned – an expedition to the Andes.

Chapter 13

The Andes were more accessible than the Himalayas, and a bit lower, and while all the main summits had been reached, many had only been climbed by the easiest route, leaving a lot of untouched faces and ridges. Calvin researched the possibilities by scouring climbing magazines and the alpine journals of different national mountaineering associations – the publications where first ascents are recorded.

We hoped to do a mixture of first ascents and established climbs. I left all that to him and helped with organising our food supply for the six weeks we'd be in the mountains. Once again we would be leaving at the start of June, and once again I got unpaid leave for the last month of the school year. Joss Lynam was a member of this expedition too, and his organisational skills were invaluable.

Climbers usually come in twos: one to lead and one to belay (taking turns), and on this trip Joss's partner was to be Dermot Somers. Dermot, a writer and member of Dal Riada since its earliest days, was the intellectual of the group. His background was similar to mine: a middle-class Catholic home where education was highly prized. He had a passionate love for the Irish language and for traditional Irish music, and he often brought his tin whistle with him on climbing trips.

The other members of the group were all Dubliners. Emmett Goulding, Harry O'Brien and Tom Hand had all been members of the Spillikin Club and were among the experienced climbers I had looked up to when I was a novice. Now they were all married with young children and had joined our club, Dal Riada. Tommy Irving was the youngest of the team at twenty-one. A keen weightlifter in his teens, he had then taken up climbing and had immediately emerged as a formidable talent.

On this trip, Calvin and I would climb together some of the time but for any particularly ambitious ascents, Tommy Irving and Calvin would be the best match and I would climb with Tom Hand. Tom, a rent collector for Dublin County Council, was a fan of satirical novelist Flann O'Brien and, like O'Brien, had a laconic wit that could puncture bombast and pretension to great comic effect.

Freeze-dried food had recently become available in the States, and as our flight went via Miami we stopped off en route to buy supplies at a climbing shop. When we arrived in Lima we had one day in which to buy the rest of our food for the mountains. I knew exactly what was available in the city, and in which stores and how much it would cost, as I'd been in touch with a nun who lived there.

Sister Ana Maria Mulqueeny was the sister of a teaching colleague of Bairbre's. My father's passion for education had influenced five of the seven of us to become teachers, and Bairbre was now working in an all-Irish girls' secondary school in south County Dublin. Sister Ana was part of a small group of Irish nuns, the Missionary Sisters of Saint Columban, who worked with the poor of Lima. In answer to my queries she wrote a friendly reply giving me details of where we could shop and added that while food in Lima was about half the price it would be in Ireland, wages were only one-tenth. She commented that we must be both very brave and very mad to be attempting to climb high mountains, and she invited us to visit her when we got to Peru.

What she didn't say was that Libertad, the area of the city where she lived, was a dangerous slum, and we couldn't persuade any taxi driver to bring us there. We finally got one driver to agree, but he did so only on condition that some of the others would come along as security. Tommy, with his weightlifter's physique, was a perfect extra passenger, and Harry O'Brien was the other volunteer. Harry, a bearded electrician who worked in the Guinness brewery, implied bulk without carrying any. Talkative, warm and with an unquenchable interest in his fellow humans, he was always a reassuring presence.

It was dark, and the taxi driver was increasingly unhappy as we drove up steep unsurfaced roads lit only by bonfires edged with shadowy figures. When we saw a sign for Libertad, we turned off into a maze of streets that were lined with little hovels. 'Libertad!' spat the driver, and he drove on cautiously until he spotted a group of children. He rolled down his window and shouted, 'Las Madres de San Columbano? Dónde están?' The children erupted in excitement and shouted 'Si, si, aquí' and ran to bang on the door of one of the small breeze-block dwellings. 'El convento!' one of them announced.

Sister Ana Maria and her companion Sister Teresa made us very welcome. Their modest home was clean and comfortable, but tiny. In their soft Irish accents they told us a bit about their mission to help the families around them. There were just five nuns in their little community, and their work ranged from education and health to prison visits. It was Sister Joan who did the prison work, but she wasn't there that day. I dreaded to think what the prisons must be like, given the living conditions in the slums themselves, but it was obvious that these nuns led happy busy lives and had no desire for anything else. They gave us tea and biscuits and asked us about our climbing plans.

We couldn't stay long as the taxi driver was waiting outside with his engine running. He wouldn't listen to the nuns' assurances that we'd all be quite safe. As we left, our taxi swerving between potholes and piles of rubble, I looked back at the two women who were waving us off: two middle-aged ladies in neat grey skirts and sensible cardigans who wouldn't have looked out of place in an Irish Countrywomen's Association craft class. Here was real courage, I thought, and it was one of the few times in my adult life when I felt proud of my Irish Catholic heritage.

Three years after our visit, the little community suffered a shocking loss. Sister Joan Sawyer, the nun who had chosen prison visits as her particular ministry, had the misfortune to be caught up in an attempted jailbreak. She was taken hostage, and when the authorities opened fire on the escaping prisoners she was shot dead along with seven other hostages. A street was named after her, and a lot of baby girls were christened Juanita in her honour.

We travelled north-east of Lima to the Cordillera Blanca range and set up our base camp in a valley lined with ice-frosted peaks. The valley was just one day's walk from the nearest road, and we transported our food and gear up it with the help of Pedro, a local man who had a string of donkeys. We pitched our tents near a green lake where there were two little stone huts roofed with straw and branches. The huts belonged to Pedro and he agreed to stay on as camp minder – a necessary precaution because a popular hiking trail ran through the valley. He would sleep in one hut and let us use the other as a kitchen. He also had a small plot of potatoes and supplied us with knobbly purple spuds as well as fish that he caught in the lake.

We had to acclimatise before we could think of climbing. Having come up from Lima, at sea level, to the base camp at 3,800 metres in just three days, we were feeling the effects of altitude. These were mainly headaches and nausea, which disappeared in a day or so. For the first few days we explored the valley and the approaches to different peaks and came back to the camp each evening. Our base – the two small stone huts and our four tents, all enclosed by a circular stone wall – was like a medieval monastic settlement. We weren't far from the Equator, and with twelve long hours of darkness, we appreciated the kitchen as a place to come together at night.

The kitchen hut had no windows and no door, and the roof was too low to allow us to stand up straight, but it gave good shelter once we'd strung a big sheet of plastic over the entrance. Joss was our cook, and the two paraffin-burning Primus stoves that he set up at the back of the hut gave a warm focus in the gloom. He made excellent chapatis (a skill he'd picked up in India as a young man) and was always scrupulously fair about dividing out the food. Dinner might be five small potatoes and part of a trout and for dessert he'd spoon a tinned peach and some syrup into each person's mug.

There was never quite enough food, but as the slightest person there I didn't find it too much of a hardship. We each had our own supply of Cadbury's Dairy Milk chocolate bars, and it was a struggle to save them for the climbs.

'What the hell is this?' It was Harry's voice, and he leaned over to hold his fork up to the nearest candle. 'Ah fuck, it's a maggot!'

'Probably fell from the thatch in the roof,' suggested Emmett, but then someone turned on a head torch, and in the swivelling light we all checked our plates. The little hut exploded. 'Shit!'

'That's disgusting!'

'Did I eat some of that?'

The little purple potatoes on every plate were full of well-boiled maggots.

Only Joss was unperturbed. 'More protein!' he declared and continued eating. The rest of us headed for our tents and the Cadbury's Dairy Milk bars.

Most of our Andean climbs began with tortuous slogs up steep loose gullies where the tip of every sprout of vegetation had a spike on it. We slipped, lurched and tottered under our heavy rucksacks, and the sweat poured off us. We were soon dehydrated and grumpy – you could never carry enough water – and were always on the lookout for a stream. Whenever we came across running water, meltwater from the glaciers higher up, everything changed. We'd dump our rucksacks and rummage for the Bird's Apeel. This was a fruit-flavoured powder that we had got free as a form of sponsorship. It wasn't bad, and we drank it cold or hot throughout the day. But it didn't compare with tea. Someone would always put a brew on, and by the time we each had a mug of tea in our hands we'd be feeling human again.

On the second day of any ascent, after a bivouac near a stream, we'd reach the snowline and find ourselves at the edge of an ocean of *nieves penitentes*. These were surreal jagged waves of ice about a metre high. *Nieves* are typical of the snow on mountains near the Equator where they have been sculpted by the hot days and freezing nights. Named for their similarity to rows of kneeling penitents, they were hard to get through. We had to step over each frozen crest in turn and down into the space (often a patch of bare earth) between it and the next one. Higher up, the snow surface evened out and we made better time.

We got to the top of one peak, Kuriikashajana (5,500 metres), but on others we were turned back by loose rock or overhanging ice. When Calvin and Tommy headed up the unclimbed North Face of Caraz II, they had to negotiate a way through huge *nieves penitentes* and said they felt like ants labouring over a giant tilted egg box. But they made it to the top, and this first ascent was a notable success for our expedition.

Each ascent, or attempt at an ascent, took two or three days of hard effort, and then we would spend a few days recovering at base camp. I had books to read and a diary to write.

> *21 June 1980*
>
> Emmett showed us male and female bitterns on the lake. Dermot is playing 'Cath Chéim an Fhia' on his tin whistle. Sitting here in base camp, feelings vary between 'it's a marvellous holiday', 'what a place to spend one's days', with an exciting route in the planning, but as well . . . fear of the blackness of an accident or death that may be lurking just beyond that ridge.

And then we would gear up again, physically and psychologically, for another sortie.

Six of us set out to climb Artesonraju: Tommy Irving and Tom Hand, Emmett Goulding and Harry O'Brien, and Calvin and myself. Dermot and Joss went to attempt a different peak. At 6,025 metres, Artesonraju was one of the highest mountains in the area. It was very impressive and was said to be the mountain featured in the Paramount Pictures banner. It was an attractive objective even though our route up its north ridge wouldn't be a first ascent.

We were making steady progress on a steepening snow slope about halfway up the mountain when we came to a wall of ice rising straight out of the snow. It was high and steep and smooth, and there was no way around it.

'I'll give it a go,' said Tommy, slipping his rucksack off and dropping it in the snow.

Tommy Irving was a skilled climber and tough as nails. Freed from the weight of his sack, he powered up the wall, kicking in with the points of his crampons and sending showers of ice splintering from the picks of his axes.

I wouldn't do that, I thought. It must be something to do with being male: that you'd throw yourself at such an obstacle without hesitation.

After about 20 metres he reached a depression in the ice and disappeared from view. A few minutes later, he hauled up his rucksack and threw the rope down for us to climb up in turn. We each stopped in surprise when we got level with him. We had expected to see a shallow cave in the ice, but Tommy had climbed into the mouth of a big opening: a natural passageway that ran back into a light-filled chamber. And there he sat, on a carpet of soft snow, taking the rope in.

The chamber was big enough for all six of us to walk around comfortably. At the back of it an easy-angled ramp rose between gleaming glassy walls and opened out onto the sunlit slope above. This hidden passageway gave us access to the upper part of the mountain. It was a magical place and a perfect spot to bivouac before heading for the summit. We untied our ropes and dropped our helmets and crampons in the snow. With a level surface to sleep on, a domed ceiling and protection from the wind, this was a five-star bivouac.

But it was cold. We were at an altitude of about 5,500 metres, and it was very cold. Calvin and I took off the outers of our double boots and quickly got into our sleeping bags with everything else still on: inner boots, jackets, overtrousers, gaiters, gloves and balaclavas. The light bivy tent gave us another thin layer of comfort, but soon the inside of it was coated with ice where our breaths had frozen. Calvin sorted that out by propping the fabric up with ice axes to keep it off our faces.

I fumbled for a while with the little zip at the back of the tent, clumsy in my two pairs of gloves, but when I got it open all the clean snow I could want was within easy reach. It takes two or three potfuls of melted snow to give one pot of water, and soon our little gas stove was purring away and warming us up. We sat back and stretched our legs. 'Ah sure where else would you be?' asked Calvin with a grin. *Where else indeed*, I thought happily. 'How's it going lads?' he shouted into the dark and got a cheerful string of mild obscenities in reply. That was Harry. He was always lively company, and his conversation was so peppered with F-words that neither he nor the rest of us ever noticed it anymore.

His companion, Emmett, would keep his thoughts to himself. Quiet and self-contained, Emmett had a natural modesty that never hinted at his achievements as Ireland's foremost alpinist. When Calvin had met English climbers in the Lake District back in 1965, the only Irish climber they'd heard of was Emmett Goulding, and they'd wanted to know who this bloke was who was doing all the hard climbs in the Alps.

In the other tent, Tom Hand would have something to say in due course, in his considered dry manner, while young Tommy Irving would just listen and smile and get busy putting a brew on. Water doesn't boil properly at altitude so tea is never quite right, but it's still a priority. The second pot of meltwater was for our freeze-dried food. I stirred the warm water into the powdery mix in its foil packet, and the comforting smell of beef stew filled the air.

We got ready to leave at 3 a.m. next morning. We wanted to reach the summit before the snow softened in the sun. I'd kept my outer boots tucked inside my sleeping bag to stop them freezing, but they were cold even before I'd finished tying the laces and my fingers started to go numb while I was fastening the straps of my crampons. We were the last pair to leave and waited in the moonlight as the others climbed the slope above the exit from the ice chamber.

We stood roped up and ready for battle: harnesses tightly buckled, head torches clipped to helmets and an ice axe in each gloved fist. This was it – the summit day. Excitement and apprehension chased each other round my imagination and my stomach.

When we got moving, the steady rhythm of swinging our axes and kicking our crampons warmed us up, and the stiffness of the night in the cramped bivy tent soon wore away. We climbed three pitches of mixed ice and snow to get to a big shoulder, and by then it was broad daylight. The ice wasn't too steep, and the ice screws went in securely but in a few sections we came across bad snow that was just a thin soft layer over a honeycomb of fragile ice.

The final ridge took us another couple of hours, and then the angle eased and we could see the others waiting for us at the summit. They had pulled a bivy tent over themselves as protection from the bitter wind. We swapped quick congratulations, and they began to set up the abseil while we stepped onto the final little rise. Then a kiss – a crush of hoods and snow goggles – and we hurried back to begin the descent.

Our direct abseil descent route would take us halfway down a big snow slope, and then we'd traverse to the side to regain the ridge we'd climbed on the way up. Once the abseil rope was in place, young Tommy Irving set off down, and Harry followed as soon as the rope was free. I went to take a photograph of Tom Hand as he clipped onto the rope but then saw that I'd run out of film. When it was my turn, I looked down and saw that Tommy and Harry had already finished a third abseil and that Tom was descending to join them. They were now halfway down the big summit snow slope and Emmett wouldn't be long after them. I'd better get a move on.

Suddenly someone was tumbling, a ball of colour, down the lower half of the huge face. 'One of them's fallen!' I yelled to Calvin and looked back in horror: would that person come tight on the rope in a sudden jerk? Would the other three be whipped off also if they were all roped together? But then I saw that one person, that one little figure, disappear over the edge way way below. He hadn't been attached to any rope.

It was Tom Hand who had fallen. The snow under his feet had collapsed when he put his weight on it, just as he came off the end of the abseil rope. He would have been leaning back with most of his weight on the rope as he abseiled down, and then, getting to the little flat spot where the others were standing, he'd have straightened up and adjusted his weight to stand and unclip from the rope. Immediately, just as he disconnected from the rope, the patch of snow beneath his boots had given way. Snow that had looked solid was rotten. He lost his balance and tumbled – all in the space of a second.

Calvin and I looked down in disbelief at the three little figures left below. They were over 100 metres lower than us, and we had to get down to them. Until we did we couldn't begin to believe what we had just seen happen. We concentrated hard on the mechanics of the rope-work for the three abseils, checking and double-checking the gate locks on our karabiners and blocking everything else from our minds.

Once the five of us were together in the middle of the big snow slope, we struggled to take in what had happened. There were bursts of talk and sudden silences. We looked with horror down the line of fall, knowing there was a huge drop below the slope. There were some rocky ledges on the lower part of the slope, and Tommy abseiled down to search them, but it was clear to all of us that Tom must have continued falling from the jutting lip to the very bottom of that north-east face, a drop of about 1,000 metres. We slanted back over to the ridge and made our way down, limbs shaking, eyes sliding away from the distress we saw on each other's faces. When we got to the snow cave, we found the place in ruins. The roof of the ice chamber had collapsed since the morning, and there was a grotesque jumble of huge blocks where we had been sleeping.

It was too late to go on, so we spent the night there, the ice dome now open to the sky. We continued on down at first light and arrived at base camp in the late evening to find that Dermot and Joss weren't back yet. Seeing how worn out the five of us were, Pedro volunteered to contact them. He walked up the valley until he spotted the light of their head torches indicating their bivouac site high up on one side of the valley. He shouted and flashed his light, and they understood that there had been a calamity. They arrived back at base camp later that night.

The next morning, Joss, Harry and I walked out to the nearest town to ring Helen, Tom's wife, and to notify the police. It would take us a full day to get to a phone – a full day before the blight of the fall would reach as far as Dublin. I had been climbing with Tom on and off over the previous few weeks, and the conversation had always flowed easily between us. He could be hilariously funny on what he saw as the foibles of human nature and the absurdities of life in general, but his natural cynicism had taken a bit of a shaking since he had become a father.

At the time of the Andean trip he was still just getting used to the unexpected pleasures of parenthood. One day when we were chatting he stopped suddenly. 'What's the date? I nearly forgot! It's Deirdre's birthday today – she's four.' His little boy, Willie, was just five months old.

Helen wasn't at home when we rang, and my parents didn't answer the phone either – they were out celebrating their thirtieth wedding anniversary but I hadn't remembered the date. It fell to a friend of Joss's to break the news to Helen and to Tom's family. When we spoke to Helen the next day, she told us that she wanted the body to rest where it lay – that she and Tom had discussed this possibility. The others spent two days searching the tangled wilderness of ice walls and crevasses below the north-east face, but they never found Tom's body. Remote, wild and not on the way to any climb, he lies there undisturbed.

Tom's death hit us hard. Calvin and I had known him for years, and he and I had climbed together in the Alps the previous summer. Harry and Emmett had been good friends of his for decades, and we all felt a burden of guilt for Helen and for the children. They hadn't chosen any of this, and the shock and loss for Helen, and for Tom's family, were compounded by there being no body to bury and no grave for the children to visit in the years to come.

As for climbing generally? We didn't feel the need to reassess our own passion for it any more than we had after Sé's death. We accepted that risk was part of mountaineering, as every climber did. Tom had been unlucky. It was as simple and as awful as that.

Chapter 14

The following year, in the summer of 1981, Calvin and I made a big move. We left Ireland, not sure if it would be for one year or much longer. We decided on North America because we wanted to spend time in the rock climbers' Mecca of Yosemite Valley in California and to ice-climb in the Canadian Rockies. In between we hoped to explore as many other climbing areas as possible, in both the USA and Canada, and to look for work. We had savings to last us three or four months, and we had let our house, which took care of the mortgage repayments.

When I gave in my notice at school, the principal wished me luck but said I might find it hard to get a job when I came back as the country was heading into a recession and there was a surplus of teachers building up. When I had begun teaching seven years before I hadn't even needed an interview; it was enough that I was qualified and that the priest manager knew I came from a respectable local family. I didn't care about my future prospects as a teacher. I was finding the job tedious and wasn't sure I'd ever go back to it. Calvin was considering training to be a mountain guide, but in the meantime he had been working as an instructor in the Tiglin Adventure Centre and he didn't hesitate to give that job up either.

We headed first to Canada, to the western city of Calgary. We chose it because it was near the Rockies and jobs were said to be plentiful there. The Stampede, the annual rodeo, was just finishing up when we arrived, and the place was full of swaggering cowboys and down-at-heel Indians (nobody was referring to them as Native Americans yet). Within a day or two, all signs of the Wild West had vanished as the city reverted to its true identity: the brash modern capital of Canada's oil-exploration industry.

We called to a climbing shop to meet kindred spirits and to flick through the local climbing guidebooks. On the shop's noticeboard, in among the 'Lost and Found', 'Gear for Sale' and 'Climbing Partners Wanted', we spotted an ad for a job: 'Two experienced rock climbers needed for oil-exploration work in the mountains. Easy work, long hours, hourly rate negotiable.'

Calvin soon had the company's boss persuaded that we were just the pair for the job. He negotiated a mountain guide's rate of $75 a day for each of us – an unbelievable amount to us – and it didn't matter that I was female. Neither did it matter that we didn't have work visas as nobody else had applied for the job.

We were to be based in the Rockies near Nordegg, an old mining town about five hours' drive north of Calgary, and would be ferried to the work site each day by helicopter. On our first morning, the pilot flew up to a narrow ridge and then let the craft plummet down the steep cliff on the far side. 'I always do that when it's people's first day,' he laughed. We strained back in our seats, grins frozen on our faces, and said nothing. He circled round and back up and landed on the edge of the ridge at the top of the cliff. 'We're at about 8,500 feet here,' he said (2,590 metres). 'If you see a thunderstorm coming in – happens a lot in the afternoons – you better get the hell outta here.'

We scrambled down onto the rock, pulling our rucksacks after us, and he roared off. He was soon back with a big orange bag swinging below the helicopter. This held the cable we would be working with. Once we had unhooked it, we hunkered down on the clifftop as he gave us a thumbs up and whirled away. In the gathering stillness it was just us and the Rockies – 60, 70, 100 miles of them in every direction. There was no snow, just a wilderness of dry limestone peaks rising out of a sea of evergreens. All of the mountains had the same characteristic shape. On one side, a boulder-strewn slope would rise from the trees and run up at an easy angle to a summit ridge. Then there would be an abrupt change of terrain as the other side of the mountain dropped away in a big vertical cliff.

Somewhere behind us, way below, a group of workers was labouring through the trees. The helicopter had dropped bags of cable at intervals along a track in the forest and the workers were unpacking it, one section from each bag, and stretching it out along the trail. The seismic cable was of heavy black rubber with a core of electronic wires, and the sections ended in metal connection points so that they could be joined to form a line hundreds of metres long. The line would eventually reach up to where we stood and over the mountaintop. It was up to us to ensure that a big awkward cliff wasn't going to be an obstacle. This was modern-day prospecting, and we were there to help force this little strip of the earth's crust to give up the secrets of its oil and gas.

It was all done with shock tactics. What began as a line drawn across a map in an office in downtown Calgary became a straight gash in a remote forest. A bulldozer would crush a rough roadway through the trees, squashing branches under its caterpillar tracks. Then came the slashers – men with chainsaws – who tidied the branches back. Next came the 'jug hounds', the small army of foot soldiers who moved down the line connecting the lengths of cable and attaching sets of geophones (jugs) to them like centipede legs and sticking the pointed metal geophones into the ground. When all of the cable was in place and connected up, underground explosions were set off, and the geophones recorded the resulting tremors. This was the core of the work. The recorded pattern of seismic activity became a valuable underground map for the client oil company. Our job was to ensure that there was no break in the miles of cable, even where it ran straight over a cliff.

The work on the mountain wasn't easy. The limestone was loose in places and shattered by frost. In spite of Calvin's expertise with equipment and ropes, it took us a lot of time to set up anchors so that we could abseil safely and secure the heavy cable to the cliff as we inched it down. We hauled ourselves back up for a lunch break and felt giddy as we calculated that we'd already earned enough to live in Yosemite for a full week. In Yosemite National Park we would be staying in a cheap campsite, and our only costs would be the camping fees and food.

After about nine hours, and no thunderstorms, the helicopter came to pick us up. Within fifteen minutes we were back at the town and settling into a motel that was full of men from other oil-exploration outfits, the names of their mineral-resource companies printed on their baseball caps. Our room had its own toilet and shower and even a kitchenette. A sign said there was a daily chambermaid service, and our dusty rucksacks were already looking guilty in the corner. We were delighted with the colour TV and its dozen channels, having only a black-and-white one at home, but then we discovered that every channel was showing the wedding of Charles and Diana and nothing else.

I was puzzled to find that all the spoons in the kitchenette's cutlery drawer were blackened – chambermaid service notwithstanding. 'They must use them for drugs,' said Calvin, noting the burn marks on the bottom of them. 'I suppose they just got tired of replacing them.'

There was good news in the restaurant: our work crew would be getting a 'hot shot': an extra payment of $10 a day for food. That was on top of our free accommodation. We treated ourselves to a good meal and a couple of beers that night, but from then on we lived frugally and took away enough food from the free breakfast every morning to keep us going throughout the day.

When the pilot dropped us on the ridge the second morning, we got a shock: all of our anchors had been vandalised, and the tattered slings fluttered ominously in the light breeze. Our day's work was ruined. We looked around uneasily, and Calvin picked up a bit of sling. 'Marmots!' he said with relief. We didn't see any of the big furry rodents, but we spotted their droppings which we were familiar with from the Alps. They had gnawed through the fabric of all the looped slings of our anchor points, attracted by the salty sweat and oil from our fingers. We had to order in new slings and wear gloves from then on.

It took us a week to fix the cable down the cliff, and then we went to work with the rest of the crew in the lowlands. As jug hounds we were paid much less, but it really was easy work and long hours, and now we were paid by the hour. The young men we worked with were a friendly bunch of Calgarians who smoked dope all day and drank all night and never brought any food out with them for our twelve-hour shifts. Sometimes Calvin lit a small fire at lunchtime, and they'd all crowd around while he cooked hotdogs for everyone.

We often got separated as we worked on different parts of the cable and kept in touch with two-way radios. Everyone said they loved hearing our brogues on the radio, and a couple of the youths swore that one of these days they were going to come over to Ireland and close those concentration camps and help us kick the Brits out. We guessed they meant the internment camps in the North where suspected IRA sympathisers had been held without trial during the early to mid 1970s.

This was the summer of 1981, the summer when ten Republican prisoners died on hunger strike in the Maze prison in Belfast. The horror and drama of their deaths had reignited the interest of the world media in the cause of a united Ireland, and these young Canadians had obviously seen and heard enough on television to have a simplistic understanding of what was a very complicated conflict. We didn't confuse them by explaining that Calvin was actually a Protestant from the Loyalist Shankill Road – a baddie by definition – and just smiled our vague appreciation instead.

One day, I was working on my own on a section of cable when I heard a sudden crashing in the trees. I reached for my radio in case it was a bear. Everyone knew that grizzlies are very dangerous but that black or brown bears aren't too much of a threat, unless you get between a mother and her cubs. But would you have time to establish all the relevant facts? It wasn't a bear that broke cover but a big bull moose. It ambled onto the track in front of me, and I had to shout and wave my arms around to chase it away before the recording engineer came on the radio to complain. Deer and longhorn sheep were common in the forest, but it was only moose that were heavy enough to cause troublesome vibrations and interfere with the line. The moose disappeared into the trees with surprising agility.

Apart from the recording engineers, there was a wide variety of workers on every prospect – slashers, drillers, shooters, 'cat' drivers, truck drivers, helicopter pilots and technicians – and they were all more highly skilled and better paid than the jug hounds. Chris, the radio operator, was based on top of a nearby mountain where he could get a clear radio signal, and one day when a technical hitch paused the work for a while we hiked up to see him.

We found him lounging in the sun outside his hut. This was a red metal box that had been airlifted onto the summit of the mountain and tied down with cables. It was called the doghouse and he was dropped off there every morning by helicopter. He had a hammock strung up inside the hut and explained how he always had to get into the hammock during thunderstorms to avoid being electrocuted. 'Man, you should see me getting bounced around in that thing when a storm hits!' he laughed and brought us outside to run our fingers over the lightning scars in the red metal walls.

When the seismic job ended, we got a few weeks' work building houses in Canmore, about an hour west of Calgary. I was up on a roof one day, hammering nails, when I suddenly realised that it was the first of September and that this would be my first autumn away from a classroom since the age of four. I was in no rush to get back to any classroom. The Rockies filled the horizon, the sun was shining, and we were earning good money.

The builder was a friendly, chatty bloke who insisted on buying us lunch a few times. On the day the job ended he was still chatty when he mentioned that he would be paying us just half of what he had originally agreed, seeing that we were working illegally. Calvin immediately said that we'd report him for employing people illegally, and underpaying them. He paid, and we left.

We bought a second-hand car with our earnings from the seismic work and the construction job. It wasn't exactly what we were looking for, being a sporty Pontiac LeMans, but it was cheap. The first time we drove out in it towards the Rockies, with our tent and climbing gear in the boot, the exhaust fell off, there were oil and fuel leaks, and the starting motor seized up. We got towed back to the garage where the guy just shrugged and gave us a quote for the repairs. After spending a fortune getting it fixed we headed south to Yosemite.

At the US border we requested three-month visitor visas and had to show 'sufficient funds' by producing our cash and Thomas Cook travellers' cheques. When you bought the travellers' cheques in the Thomas Cook office in Westmoreland Street in Dublin, they came in a neat blue plastic wallet, the cheques on one side and the page with the list of their serial numbers on the other. The $50 cheques were a pleasingly official-looking light green and had your name already printed on them and a space for your signature below. There was also a printed warning that the list of the serial numbers should be kept separate from the cheques so you could get them cancelled and replaced 'in the event of loss or theft'.

Some English climbers in Calgary had given us a tip about the cheques: ring the Thomas Cook emergency number, say we'd lost our cheques and ask for them to be cancelled and replaced, giving the list of serial numbers. The company sent us out another set, and then both lots, looking equally valid, could be shown to the immigration officials. There was a nice symmetry to being able to double our apparent wealth as we knew we could easily live for three months on half of what it would cost ordinary tourists. The worthless cheques passed muster for us at US and Canadian immigration four times so it was a good tip, as long as we were never stupid enough or careless enough to attempt to cash the cancelled ones.

We rolled south through the outsized alien landscapes of Montana, Idaho, Nevada and California, driving all day and pulling into lay-bys at night to sleep in the car. Breakfast was the best part of the day. The first time we ordered breakfast in a diner, the waitress brought us plates piled high with eggs over-easy, bacon, sausages and hash browns, plus pancakes with maple syrup and cream. As the maple syrup swirled around the oozing egg yolks, we saw that they did food differently over here. 'Have a nice day!' the waitress chirped as we left. We'd never heard that before and were startled by its insistent cheeriness.

It was in the cafeteria in Yosemite village that we saw obese people for the first time. An endless stream of day visitors would move slowly along the self-service counters, filling their trays with Coke, salad, burgers, fries, desserts and enormous dripping slices of red watermelon. They left a lot of food behind, and a predatory climber might commandeer their tray when they left. Having been brought up to finish everything on my plate, with the constant reminder that waste was sinful because there were poor starving children in Africa, I thought that this careless attitude to abundant food was immoral.

One day in the cafeteria we heard a woman's voice rising with outrage. 'Excuse me, but what are you doing? That's our food!' The woman was glaring at someone at the next table. She had just come back from the restroom with her young daughter and had found a scruffy climber helping himself to the food on her tray. 'Oh, sorry about that, ma'am,' he said, making for the door. He got away with it that time, but 'scarfing' (eating food left behind by someone else) was against the law, and the authorities viewed it as a type of stealing. Climbers living on a few dollars a day were not a fastidious lot – some even used the already-used knives and forks to tuck in with, but you had to be discreet.

Outside of the cafeteria our food was basic because the general store was very expensive. Every so often we'd drive out of Yosemite National Park to stock up on cheap provisions at the nearest town, but then there was the problem of storing the food in the campsite. Yosemite Valley is an overpopulated little pocket in the vast wilderness of the Sierra Nevada mountains, and there are hungry critters on every side. Raccoons were the biggest nuisance. A friend left food in his zipped-up tent, and a raccoon chewed its way in through one wall and out through the other. There were horizontal wire cables above every camping site, and campers were obliged to keep their food high on the wire, out of the reach of bears.

You had to divide your food into two bags that would counterbalance each other when they were tied together and tossed over the high wire.

It often took two people to get them down again: one to dislodge them with a big stick and the other to catch them. One night we were woken by a loud noise outside the tent. 'A bear! It must be a bear at the food!' said Calvin, and he got out to investigate. A minute later I heard his urgent whisper: 'Clare, quick! Come and see this!'

I was slow to leave my sleeping bag. Wrestling with bears was Calvin's department. The clearing in the pine trees was bright in the moonlight and I could see the gleam of the wire and the dark shapes of the food bags hanging below it. Then I saw a third shape and a sudden movement: a bear cub was scrabbling out along the wire, trying to grab at the bags. But where was the mother? Then we saw her: a big shadowy creature, halfway up the tree nearest to the cable. Before we realised what they were at, the deed was done. The cub had batted the string of the bigger bag so that it swung right over to the mother, and she had grabbed it and pulled it free. The other bag fell to the ground, and the cub, frightened now that it had seen us, peed straight down on top of it. In a crashing of undergrowth, the two of them disappeared with their booty.

In the morning, we followed their trail in the hope of salvaging something for breakfast. Their route through the pines was well marked with orange peels, eggshells and wavering lines of porridge oats and pancake mix. Deeper into the forest we came across the empty tins and jars and food packets that marked the site of their picnic. The mother had run a sharp claw around the tops of the tins of tomatoes and refried beans, and the perfect metal discs were left lying among the pine needles. She had unscrewed the lids of the jars of honey and jam and licked them clean. The bears had eaten everything except our ground coffee and the precious Red Rose teabags that we had brought from Canada. We rescued half a box.

Yosemite drew climbers from all over the world. Its glacier-carved valley had walls of superb granite that provided rock climbing of the highest quality. It also had an excellent climate, and we came out of hibernation under its Californian sun. We felt strong and fit on the warm rock and could climb day after day without worrying about the weather. The cracks we slipped our hands into weren't cold and slick with green lichen as they sometimes were at home, and we never had to wipe our shoes on our trouser legs to dry them as we climbed.

It wasn't just the lifestyle. American climbers were different too. They were tall and tanned, and they 'worked out'. Some of them wore headbands and white knee socks with horizontal stripes, like college athletes. They *were* athletes, rock athletes, and they found enough on the towering walls of this narrow valley to feed their obsessions. They didn't look to the high snowy mountains that still drew the fleece-clad climbers of Britain and Ireland. Rock climbing was independent of mountaineering now, and it had come of age in Yosemite, the new centre of the climbing world.

There was a friendly community of climbers in Camp 4, the climbers' campsite. They were mainly American and English, and many of them were on extended trips like ours. There was talk of moving south to the desert crags of Joshua Tree for the winter and then on to Colorado in the spring. I was almost twenty-nine and Calvin thirty-eight, but life felt as full of possibilities as it would have if we'd still been teenagers.

We planned to stay in Yosemite for six or seven weeks so it seemed like a good place to get married. Calvin reminded me of an incident from a few years earlier, the autumn of 1978, when we had first visited the valley and he had stayed on after I went home for the new school term. He wanted to do a 'big wall' – a multi-day climb on steep rock that I found too overwhelming to contemplate – and planned to climb the Nose, the famous direct line up El Capitan. The huge monolith known as El Cap rises out of the Yosemite meadows like a great blunt ship's prow of pale grey rock. It is startlingly vertical, and its massive swell of granite sweeps up for 1,200 metres, making it one of the most impressive rock formations on the planet.

For the climb, Calvin teamed up with two English climbers, and they amassed the gear, food and water they'd need for three or four days of climbing on the wall and sleeping on ledges that were too narrow to be visible from the ground. Then one of the English climbers was arrested for shoplifting. He had stolen a bologna sausage in the general store and was taken away by two park rangers and brought before a judge. 'A $25 fine, young man, or a day cleaning the public toilets. Your choice.' The climber chose the day cleaning toilets but explained to the judge that he was planning to start up a big wall with Calvin and another mate the following day. The judge considerately deferred the sentence for four days so that the climb could go ahead. In the end, they did the route in just two and a half days, and he had time to spare for the toilet cleaning.

But now that we needed a judge to officiate at our wedding, there was none to be found. The park rangers told us that we'd have to go to the town of Merced, outside the national park, where there was a county office and a permanent judge. At the office we showed proof of identity and Calvin's divorce papers and were given a date for the civil marriage ceremony a few weeks later.

Camp 4, the most famous campsite in the climbing world, was scruffy, sociable and cheap. That made it a perfect climbers' campsite but it wasn't the best place to be getting married from. The 'bathroom' block had cold-water showers only and there were no mirrors. When we were getting ready in the tent Calvin couldn't find anything clean to wear. I had on my best jeans and a new sweater and, after rummaging in my rucksack, I dug out a clean shirt and my second-best pair of jeans for him. And then we were off, down the narrow road between the huge granite walls and out of the valley with Blondie's 'The Tide Is High' loud on the car radio.

Merced was hot and dusty and looked as if it should be in Mexico. The sun glinted sharply off the parked cars in front of the courthouse, and it was a relief to get into the air-conditioned interior. We had witnesses from home, three Belfast guys, friends of ours, who happened to be climbing in Yosemite at the same time. We were very happy to have their company. We went first into an open office where four secretaries were working. They looked up with interest, and one of them, a big black woman, swivelled round in her chair and boomed, 'Well, gal, which o' them is it gonna be?' as if all my options were still open.

We were directed into the empty courtroom to wait for the judge. There was a heavily-armed policeman at the door and a big

American flag on display, just like in the movies. The ceremony was brief. We had a ring that I'd brought from home and kept safe with the travellers' cheques in the inner lid of my rucksack. It had belonged to my grandmother and my aunt, who had never married, had given it to me before I left. She said she was afraid she might lose it. I was the one likely to lose it as I'd be living in a tent in the mountains for months on end, but I took it anyway and thanked her. And neither of us mentioned marriage. I wore it for a day or two after the wedding and then put it back in the lid of my 'sack. Rings and climbing don't go. A climber we knew left part of his finger behind on a climb in Scotland when he fell and the ring stayed jammed in a crack.

After the ceremony, our friends took a few photographs and the five of us went to an all-you-can-eat Mexican restaurant to celebrate. That evening I rang home from the public phone in the campsite. My mother was quietly relieved that we had got that out of the way, and my father was pleased. He told my aunt that we'd got married in a little Franciscan mission church in the mountains and that the slides (the photographic evidence) had got lost in the post.

A year after we were married, a teacher named Eileen Flynn was sacked from a school in County Wexford. She had been working at the Holy Faith Convent, a girls' secondary school, in the town of New Ross, and had lost her job because she was living with a separated man with whom she had had a baby. That news story must have sent secret shivers through many a staffroom. Her unforgiveable offence was that she was living openly with the separated man. I thought she must be a very brave woman. The ban on divorce was still in place, and when a constitutional referendum to lift it was put to the electorate in 1986, it was defeated 2:1.

Chapter 15

When we got married, in the autumn of 1981, we had no thoughts yet of going home. We climbed in Joshua Tree, a desert playground of granite domes in Southern California, and drove back north to Calgary when our three-month visitor visas were up. It was winter, and we skied over frozen lakes, climbed iced-up waterfalls and shared a rickety old wooden house with other climbers.

The boss of the seismic company had told us to get in touch if we needed work again, and we were delighted to find that there was a big job starting in the new year. This prospect was in northern Alberta, but it might as well have been in Siberia. We lived in prefabs in a temporary camp in the forest, and after the 5 a.m. wake-up call we put on so many clothes that it was hard to bend over to zip up our snow boots. We had ski suits as a top layer, having bought them in a thrift shop in Calgary that had a big notice over the door: 'Where good neighbours can shop with dignity.' The only suit I could find in the right size was a shiny pink one.

It was just a short dash from our trailer to the kitchen but even then your eyelashes would begin to stick together as they froze, and you'd leave skin on the metal handle of the door if your hands were damp. In the bacon-infused warmth inside, there was a lavish array of hot food on offer, all free of course. The choice at dinnertime was even more excessive, but still people complained because there was no lobster to go with the steak. The cooks didn't use a freezer but left the packages of meat and other supplies outside to freeze in the snow.

When the radio said it was going to be –38°C, with wind chill bringing it to –45°C, people just shrugged. According to Canadian work regulations, if you worked outdoors in anything below –20°C you did so at your own risk, but there were no regulations and no unions up here. There were about fifty workers in the camp, including four other young women. This was their first seismic job, and they had left dull office jobs in Calgary, lured by the promise of good pay and a ten-to-one gender imbalance. They all skipped breakfast because they were slimming and they needed time to curl their hair. We double-checked everything before heading out in the trucks: lunch, flask, spare gloves, balaclava, scarf, jacket – nothing could be left to chance. It was like going winter climbing in Scotland, where conditions are often polar, but with the extra bulky ski-suit layer making us look like Michelin men.

We were older than the average jug hound and were sometimes given more responsibility. Calvin drove a truck from the beginning, and soon I was asked to drive one too. I said no because I wasn't able to drive. 'That's OK,' said the guy managing our crew. 'It's just like driving a car.'

'No, I really can't drive. I've never even driven a car.'

He looked at me in surprise. 'Just turn the key, move the clutch into drive and off you go.'

Within an hour I was driving a truck through the snow while two helpers flung sets of geophones off the back. It wasn't too bad – the vehicle was automatic, and it was warm in the cab.

We worked in an endless forest of skimpy ragged trees that crowded each side of the freshly-cut track. It was flat muskeg country, swampy and alive with mosquitoes in summer, but in winter it froze solid and the big vehicles could roll in. The rough, poorly defined tracks were full of hazards, and trucks often ended up jammed in the snowy piles of broken branches that had been bulldozed off to the side.

I had to learn how to winch other trucks out of the ditch. To rescue a stranded truck you had to attach a winch from your truck to the front of the other one and then, from inside the cab, activate an electric motor to draw it in. The cab didn't promise much protection should the metal cable snap and come flying through the windscreen.

If your own truck got stuck, and there wasn't another vehicle in the vicinity, you had to do a self-rescue. This was a lot more nerve-wracking. You had to select the healthiest looking of the miserable trees that were within reach, pass the cable around it, hook it back to the front of your truck, hop in, switch the winch motor on and sit, hands clamped to the steering wheel, as the cable squealed and the tree groaned and the truck shuddered itself free. On days like that the winter pay of $50 a day didn't seem like very much after all.

We ate our lunch in the truck cab, squashed in with others who soon felt like friends. The girls had given up curling their Princess Diana hair – it got ruined under their caps anyway – but they never stopped skipping breakfast. They worked hard, dragging cables over frozen lakes and stamping the flat-headed spikes of the geophones into the snow. And they were stoical when they found no boyfriend material among the feckless youths all around them.

As the afternoon wore on and the cold intensified, everyone in the crew worked with an ear cocked to the nearest radio. When the call came to finish up, the long drive back would take us over the frozen Athabasca River. There was no bridge, and we drove straight across the ice. In early March, as the work was coming to an end, there were rumours of a thaw. Someone had spotted open water flowing near our crossing point. The next evening, when Calvin drove the truck across the river, we looked back and saw water pooling in the wheel ruts in the ice. Inside the crowded cab we held our breath while we rode the ice-topped river and were communally thrilled as we rattled up the far bank.

When we got back to Calgary, I filled a long letter home with an account of our weeks in the winter camp: the work, the food, the wildlife, the freezing temperatures and the shimmering blue-green curtains of the aurora borealis. My mother's letters to me were usually full of family news, what the weather was like and how the price of cigarettes had just gone up in the budget, but this time when she replied it was with an uncharacteristic note of longing: 'We wouldn't mind heading off into the wild . . . ice bridges, wolves, lynx and bobcats . . . it's just too much to take when your only excitement for the day will be cleaning the venetian blinds and defrosting the stewing beef for the dinner.' I could picture her at home, in her navy nylon housecoat. She'd be sitting at the kitchen table, smoking, the ash on her cigarette getting longer as she stared into space.

On a cold day in late March we were reading newspapers in the warmth and comfort of the Calgary public library when a headline in the *Globe and Mail* jumped out at me: 'Irish School Is a Challenge to Status Quo.' It was an account of how a new multi-denominational primary school had just opened in Bray, County Wicklow. Bray – my home town! The Bray School Project was just the second multi-denominational primary school in the history of the state to get 'national' school status. Its recognition by the Department of Education followed the official acceptance of the Dalkey School Project a few years earlier. Both schools resulted from the hard work of parents who were committed to providing families with an alternative to the sectarian ethos of all the other national schools in the country.

My father approved highly of this new development and posted me a job application when the school advertised for teachers. I flew home in June 1982 for an interview. The flight landed in Shannon, where all transatlantic flights to Ireland landed in those days, and my brother Shane was there to pick me up. As we drove through the Midlands towards Dublin, I was struck by the beauty of the countryside where soft grass graced every patch of open ground and Norman castles stood unheralded in fields of cows. And I realised that I'd be quite happy to come home again.

I was offered the teaching job in the new school and flew back to California for one last month of climbing in the sun. I brought a box of Lyons Green Label teabags with me and a six-pack of the new Guinness cans that came with a big plastic syringe. The syringe let you put a creamy head on the Guinness once you'd poured it – our friends in Camp 4 were intrigued. Calvin was happy to come home too and planned to begin his mountain guide's training.

I started teaching in the Bray School Project the following September. Now I was Mrs Torrans, a respectable married woman, though ironically no one in that liberal school community cared one way or the other.

Chapter 16

While I was settling back to teaching, Calvin was preparing for another big trip. A friend of ours, and fellow Dal Riada club member, Ian Rea, was organising an expedition to the sacred mountain of Shivling in the Indian Himalayas, and he invited Calvin along.

Ian, like Calvin, had climbing in his soul, and the rest of his existence flowed around it. At twenty-seven he was already a mountaineer's mountaineer, and the many climbs he had done in the Mournes, in Scotland and in the Alps drew considerable respect from his fellow climbers.

The previous year, in 1982, he and two other young Belfast climbers, Dawson Stelfox and Tommy Maguire, had gone to the Garwhal area of northern India where they had made the first ascent of a beautiful ice face – the previously unclimbed north face of Bhagirathi II. This was a very impressive success for the three young climbers, but they suffered a catastrophe on the descent. Tommy slipped and was badly injured when he fell hundreds of metres. He died on the mountain and was buried there by his two friends.

Shivling, Shiva's holy mountain, is the most revered peak in the Indian Himalayas. Its snows feed the Ganges river, and millions of Hindu pilgrims walk to its base every year. For climbers, the attraction lies in its shape: a graceful pyramid of rock and ice that rises to over 6,500 metres. There is no 'walk-up' route on any side, and it was only in 1974 that the summit was first reached. The remaining unclimbed faces and ridges would give hard technical climbing, climbing of the sort that Ian and his highly competent and single-minded companions dreamed of getting to grips with.

They were a team of four, and the other pair, Alan Currans and Eddie Cooper, also hailed from Belfast. Alan had been one of our witnesses when we got married in Yosemite, and Eddie was a young climbing ace who, having done all the hardest routes at Fairhead, had then put up even harder new ones of his own. They got on very well together. 'And why wouldn't we?' Calvin wrote to me. 'Four good Prods going forth for God and Ulster!'

The conditions on Shivling were difficult. High on the north-west face, heavy snowfall pinned them down in the open, without a tent, for four days. When they retreated to the bottom of the face they were glad to be able to shelter for the night inside a crevasse. After a rest back at base camp they attempted the west ridge. The climbing there was a mix of rock and snow and was of excellent quality. They made good time until they came to a major obstacle at three-quarters height: a barrier of tottering ice columns that they could find no way through.

I was shocked to see them when they came home. They looked gaunt and old, their bodies wasted by the physical effort and the inadequate food. But it had been a great trip. They'd given it their best shot and had come home friends – not something that always happens on expeditions. And they weren't too disappointed by their lack of success. They had been climbing alpine style – fast and light and without back-up – and they knew that success on such a technically challenging peak would depend, to a large extent, on luck.

Later in the summer, when Calvin had put some weight back on, we drove out to Chamonix as usual. He was scheduled to work for a few weeks on an alpine course for the Tiglin Adventure Centre, and, as we always climb in twos, I looked around for another partner from among the Irish climbers in the campsite. Some of my companions, who were all male, were better climbers than me and some were not, but whoever I was with it was always an equal partnership. It was very rare to see a woman lead climbing on a route in the Alps at that time, and whenever I appeared at the foot of a climb, there was always a presumption from Continental climbers that whoever I was with must be either a professional guide or a boyfriend, and that he would be doing all the leading.

This was the case when Donie O'Sullivan and I went to climb the West Face of the Petites Jorasses that summer. Donie, a young Dubliner, was a trainee doctor and a very good climber. Like me he caused raised eyebrows on Monday mornings when he appeared at work with small cuts on his hands after a weekend tussling with rough cracks. We both reckoned that cuts healed more quickly if left open to the air.

The Petites Jorasses, a 3,650-metre peak on the frontier ridge between France and Italy, had a hut situated below its west face, and we decided that instead of bivouacking we'd spend the night there before the climb. Alpine huts vary in size and quality and range from rough 'unguarded' cabins that provide shelter only, to large expensive establishments that cater for over a hundred people. All guarded huts provide meals and have supplies of fresh food delivered to them regularly by helicopter.

The Refuge du Leschaux was a small metal shed on a shoulder of rock above the Leschaux Glacier, three hours' slog up the Mer de Glace from the Montenvers viewing point. It looked too small to have a guardian or host, but there he was, a tough weather-beaten character who glared at us disapprovingly for arriving late and, no doubt, for cooking our own food outside the refuge instead of paying for the restaurant service that he provided. It was hard to see how this man could conjure up anything palatable in the cramped conditions of that little cabin, but doubtless he did, and, this being France, it was probably very good.

He gestured to the crowded sleeping platform in the dim interior. It was already full of men, a dozen or more of them, some settled for the night, others sitting up to sort their gear in the light of their head torches. 'There, over there in the corner. Make a couple,' the guardian growled again, in English, and handed us a couple of blankets. We squashed in. Even when sleeping in a room full of men I never felt uncomfortable in an alpine hut. Nobody really undresses, and thoughts of the coming climb are all that are on anybody's mind, as far as I know.

In the morning we set out before dawn and followed the rising glacier for a further two hours to the foot of the Petites Jorasses. The West Face was a relatively popular climb, and we were glad to find that there was no one ahead of us when we reached the *bergschrund* – the last big crevasse that gapes where the glacier peels back from the rock face. It was broad daylight now and we set about organising our gear for the move off the ice and onto the steep rock.

Just then, two French climbers arrived. They were not pleased to find that *les Anglais* had beaten them to it and, worse, that they'd be held back all day by a woman. After a brusque 'Bonjour', they smoked and chatted among themselves while we worked around them.

Bergschrunds are not nice places. The icy lip of the crevasse is never broad enough or flat enough for comfort. You teeter on each foot in turn to take off your crampons, as they won't be any use on the rock, and then sort the ropes. You tighten up your harness – *no chance of a pee now that those guys have arrived* – and clip on the rock climbing gear. You have to take great care that no glove, helmet, ice axe, karabiner or head torch tumbles into the unplumbed maw of the *bergschrund.*

I was the first to climb. I felt self-conscious starting up in front of the Frenchmen but smug too at their sudden silence when they realised that I was the one heading off to lead the first pitch. I made some moves up the initial crack and it felt hard. If I'd been in my flexible rock shoes I would have made short work of it, but my heavy alpine boots and bulky rucksack weighed me down. The rock was very cold, and then, without warning, my hands slipped. I fell and landed on the shoulders of one of the Frenchmen. He cursed as I slithered on down to the ice.

'Pardon, pardon monsieur, excusez-moi,' I gabbled, and in a welter of shame muttered, 'You'd better do it,' to Donie.

But then, for some reason, the whole atmosphere changed, and everyone relaxed. 'It's as well you didn't have your crampons on!'

laughed the Frenchman, and in the chit-chat that followed we managed to mention that we were in fact *Irlandais* and to wallow in the warmth that that little announcement always generated among French people. With some advice from Donie and 'Bon courage' from the two Frenchmen, I had another go at the crack, and this time I got up it. And the other seventeen pitches went fine.

The alpine climbing continued to go well for me in Chamonix that year, and I made a joyful entry in my diary on 16 August 1983: '6 routes so far. Great season – flying up everything!'

Chapter 17

I was thirty-one in that summer of 1983 and Calvin forty, and for the first time we felt reasonably settled. I had a permanent job in a progressive school that suited me – teaching was much more exciting now, though also much more demanding – and Calvin was ready to begin his mountain guide's training.

In the nineteenth century, the early years of alpinism, mountain guides were shepherds, hunters, crystal gatherers or farmers: people who had some knowledge of the peaks in their locality and of the changing conditions that might be found on them. By the 1980s, mountain guides, who could more accurately be called *alpine* or *international* guides, were highly trained professionals with a globally recognised qualification overseen by the International Federation of Mountain Guides Associations.

The training and assessment were tough, and only elite alpinists were accepted onto the scheme. Being a very good climber was an essential requirement, but there was also a high level of technical expertise needed in areas such as first aid, avalanche awareness and mountain rescue. And you had to be able to ski. Calvin spent Christmas on his own in Chamonix teaching himself the basics while I took up an invitation to go home to my parents.

In the huts and cable cars, guides get preferential treatment and special rates. Not only do they bring customers onto the glaciers and into the alpine huts, but their presence ensures that professional rescue is always at hand, whoever should happen to need it. Shepherding clients along narrow snow ridges or up and down steep rock faces at altitude requires quick reactions and good judgement, as well as steadiness and confidence, and Calvin had all these qualities in spades.

Guiding was the perfect profession for him, the one job that would make the most of his exceptional climbing experience and skills. His personality suited the task too as he had an easy way of inspiring confidence and giving support without ever being patronising. He was the first person on the island of Ireland to train as a mountain guide, and he qualified within the British Mountain Guides accreditation scheme as there is no Irish equivalent.

Alpine guiding was, essentially, summer work, and Calvin was glad to be offered a job with a second-level education group – the City of Dublin Vocational Education Committee – where the educational opportunities included an introduction to outdoor adventure activities. He was taken on as a temporary part-time employee, which was not ideal, but he liked the work. He, of all people, knew the value of introducing city kids to the outdoors. His summer work as an alpine guide provided a good supplement to his earnings.

It was at around this time, in the early 1980s, that we started thinking about having a family. We both wanted children but I was worried that I'd never be able to climb at the same standard again after having a baby. Would the body bounce back? I didn't know any woman who climbed as much as I did and had children. I was delighted when our GP confirmed the pregnancy, but doubts about the future kept niggling. What sacrifices would I have to make? Would I be plonked in an armchair for months on end, overweight and breastfeeding, while Calvin got his climbing gear ready? I knew I'd burn with frustration if that was how things worked out.

As the months went by, I cut down on my climbing and stopped leading altogether. I kept fit by running and hill walking, and my strong abdominal muscles prevented my shape from ever getting unwieldy. It was a late Easter that year, in 1984, and the weather was glorious when Sheila and I went on a mountaineering trip to Scotland. Sheila had remained a close friend to both Bairbre and me since we'd met in the UCD Mountaineering Club in 1971. Now working as a forensic scientist – a career in which she was to achieve international recognition – she had kept up her interest in mountaineering.

Our objective was the traverse of the famous Cuillin ridge on the Isle of Skye. The Cuillin ridge is an almost alpine extravaganza of rocky pinnacles and peaks, with one pitch of pure rock climbing, and a bivouac halfway along. We were in high spirits as we negotiated its twenty-two-summit crest, walking and scrambling by turns, and taking the rope out to secure each other on some of the steeper ascents and descents. The weather was perfect, hot even, and we were lucky to come across a few old snow patches where we could unpack our gas stove and melt snow to refill our water bottles.

Coming near the end of the ridge on the second day, I stopped to look back over the rises and dips of the long twisting spine of rock we'd traversed. We had only one more uphill, and I felt not just strong and fit but powerful. I had ten weeks to go until the baby was due and was confident that I'd take all this birth stuff in my stride.

I was a complete sucker for the natural-childbirth ideas of the time. They circulated with the moral force of religious truths. I signed up for a series of prenatal classes in Bray, which promised untold physical and spiritual rewards for you and your baby if you followed some special exercises and meditations. It turned out that I was the only one on the course, and the earnest young woman running it was so caring and nice that I never went back after the first session. I decided I might as well just stick with the advice the National Maternity Hospital in Dublin's Holles Street had to offer. In their promotion of natural childbirth, their message was that with the right breathing and the right attitude, and your partner in full attendance, you'll be grand.

But no one spoke clearly about the pain of labour, the pure physical pain whose pattern and intensity were, when the time came, well beyond anything I could control with my breathing. I was used to hard physical effort, to putting my head down and pacing myself so that I could deal with such challenges bit by bit, whether on a tough hill walk or an alpine climb or on the marathon I had run the previous year, but in labour I wasn't in control, and that was frightening.

Calvin, though squeamish, did his best to be supportive and to stick it out with me in the labour ward. Things were moving slowly, and eventually the midwife said, 'We'll give you some gas now.' I knew I should object – it wouldn't be proper natural childbirth if they gave me painkillers – but I said nothing. Inside the mask I could hear my shredded breaths amplified as I waited for the gas to take effect. It didn't. Years later I read somewhere that the gas had no pain-dulling element at all, that it was just for moving the process along. This it did, but by then Calvin had left the bedside, the midwife having asked him to go before he passed out.

It was a beautiful baby boy, and the euphoria I felt when I woke the next morning was what I had felt just twice before: when I led my first VS climb and when I had the nerve to climb through the crux of my first Extreme new route at Fairhead. But even climbing couldn't compare with the wonder of having a child. I'd found over the years that a lot of the things that women were interested in, like handbags and weddings, meant nothing to me, but this one, this great cliché of motherhood, was as marvellous and as emotionally overwhelming as everyone had said it would be.

Michael, named after my father, was a happy and undemanding child, quick to smile, like his dad. With careful planning we were able to fit him in with our climbing, but it wasn't easy. We brought him away camping when he was two weeks old. I had guessed, rightly, that it would be as easy to care for him in a small tent as it would be at home, but I hadn't bargained for the weather. We pitched our tent on a patch of grass by the shore of Glencar Lake in County Sligo, and when it started to rain heavily I realised that we'd soon run out of clean clothes for the baby as we wouldn't be able to dry anything. But it wasn't the laundry that forced us to pack up: it was the rising lake that came within inches of the tent door overnight. Two weeks later we set off for Chamonix where we met up with Irish climbing friends. Calvin managed to get one serious alpine route done, but I was happy to go walking in the woods, between feeds, and to test out my light-again body on some short climbs in the valley.

Michael was just six weeks old when I was due back at work (he had been overdue at birth), and there were never enough hours in the day. We left him with a minder while I was at school, and when I got home each afternoon, after picking him up, I'd rush around washing cloth nappies, tidying, cleaning, baking bread and making jam, in between looking after him. I wasn't house-proud but I couldn't bear disorder and housework loomed large for me – too large in retrospect. But while Calvin never noticed whether the windows needed to be cleaned or the carpet shampooed, he did do a lot of the cooking.

I was always busy. As well as the housework and constant after-hours school work, I was editing a short-lived climbing magazine for the FMCI. And I felt guilty if I didn't get out for a run every second day. I got an ache in my back and had colds for what seemed like two weeks out of every four, but I never eased up. That would have been weakness. I got back to the same fitness level for climbing – both physical and mental – that I'd had before I became pregnant, and that was a great relief. Calvin and I still climbed, weather permitting, every weekend from March to November. We would meet up with friends and take turns looking after Michael. We were usually away from Friday evening until Sunday night, and on Monday mornings in school I would be physically tired but zinging with energy after the weekend's excitement.

On the first ascent of our new route 'Eat the Peach' at Fairhead in 1986, we split the climbing and the childminding. Calvin led the first rope length, with our friend Donie, and they set up an anchor on a big ledge two-thirds of the way up the cliff. Then Calvin abseiled off and walked around to meet me: a forty-five-minute trek through the boulders at the bottom, up the big Greyman's Path gully and then along the heathery cliff rim to where I was waiting with Michael, who was almost two. When I handed Michael over, I abseiled down to Donie and led the top rope length. That top pitch turned out to be the crux, and it was respectably hard, so it was worth the hassle. That was my last new route for a while because a month later I was very happy to discover that I was pregnant again.

Our second boy, Robert, another calm and undemanding child,

was born in February 1987, and the following week I went back to the climbing wall to check what strength I had left in my arms. When Robert was three weeks old it felt like time to get back to serious training. I was totally in love with the sweet new baby, but I felt a compulsion to reassert the climber side of my identity. This was partly to show myself that I could. I never followed a structured training programme, as many climbers were now doing, but it was exhilarating to be climbing regularly and to feel my body grow leaner and stronger by the week, and to have it back under my own control again.

Training for both of us was climbing at a primitive climbing wall in a school gym and running. The first one to go for a run after work, usually Calvin, would arrive back in high spirits to stretch and be bounced on by the boys while the other (me) did some vaguely resentful warm-up exercises in the hall before forcing myself out to banish my own stresses in turn.

Now that we had a second child, there was, of course, less time than ever. The ethical cloth nappies and their special smelly soaking bucket were long gone, and we were using disposable ones like everyone else, but still the housework seemed endless. I cleaned and sorted and planned and packed the clothes for the weekend trips away and unpacked them and threw them in the wash on Sunday nights while Calvin looked after the climbing gear and dried the tent out. It was an oddly traditional female/male division of labour, but I was the one most likely to know who owned which little pair of socks while it was Calvin who'd notice if we had mislaid a couple of karabiners at the weekend. Things evened out considerably when he took over all of the cooking. He was much better at it than me, and whether he was tipping chopped garlic into a frying pan outside a small tent in Donegal or had the oven and three saucepans on the go in our kitchen in Bray, the dinners he cooked were always very good.

My father often offered to babysit for us. He regarded his grandchildren as the treasures of his old age and now that he had retired, he sometimes looked after our boys for whole weekends. My mother, on the other hand, had had enough of all that. The task of caring for her seven children had dominated her adult life, curbing her spirit and dictating the shape of each of her days. As soon as she had some time to call her own she devoted it to studying. She signed up for a course in English with the Open University and began attending classes in Italian literature, through Italian.

I sometimes felt a bit guilty about dragging Michael and Robert from pillar to post at weekends. Nights in tents or huts and days at crags would not have been their first choice, but on the plus side they had two happy parents as we were both able to continue climbing. Family life was full and busy. Calvin and I were with the boys fairly constantly outside of work hours, and we had the advantage that our formal working day was shorter than the average. That constant presence was to change over the next decade as Calvin would be absent for months at a time on four major expeditions.

In late 1988, he was invited on two forthcoming Irish expeditions to the Himalayas: one to Manaslu (Nepal) in 1991 and a second to Everest in 1993. I would have been considered as a team member for one or both of these expeditions too if I hadn't made it known that I'd lost all interest in big trips to high mountains after the children were born. I couldn't imagine being away from Michael and Robert for any length of time, even if there was someone to mind them, but I never considered cutting back on climbing generally.

Calvin shared all of the parenting with me, but I knew I'd be able to manage the boys easily enough when he was away. Our climbing was a different matter though and was not something I could do in his absence without a lot of reorganising. I reckoned that if our climbing partnership was going to be disrupted by him heading off to climb some of the greatest giants of the Himalayas – he was already in training for the 1989 British Makalu (8,485 metres) expedition to Nepal and now had these invitations for Manaslu (8,163 metres) and Everest (8,848 metres) – it would be the perfect time for me to commit to the super-productive project of having another baby.

Chapter 18

I was three months pregnant when Calvin headed off to Nepal at the beginning of August 1989. This was for the Makalu expedition, and he wasn't due home until the beginning of November. Three weeks passed, and all I'd had from him was a single postcard from Kathmandu. Then one evening when I bundled in with the boys and the bags of shopping, my heart jumped to see two foreign-looking letters on the hall mat.

Climbers sending letters home from Himalayan base camps sometimes gave them to passing trekkers to post in remote villages. Surprisingly, most of the letters made it. Now two blue aerogrammes had arrived together, their flimsy folds stiffened up by the oversized Nepalese stamps. Each of the letters was just a single translucent sheet, but they were covered all over with Calvin's spidery writing and mad spelling. Full of the sights and sounds of Kathmandu, they were full too of his love. They made me laugh and cry as I counted the days until he'd be home again.

The invitation to join the 1989 British Blackspur Makalu Expedition was a great opportunity for Calvin. He was forty-six but still in his climbing prime. It's said that while your twenties are the best years for climbing in the Alps, your forties are the best for the Himalayas as it's only then that you have the stamina, experience and judgement needed for the big peaks. And Makalu was a big peak. It was the fifth-highest in the world and was considerably higher than any mountain yet attempted by any Irish expedition.

Calvin wrote about his eight teammates and about the dozens of porters they had to hire to carry the food needed for their three months at base camp. He described how their two-week-long trek had brought them from hot and humid foothills through leech-infested rainforests and up to the cold and windy highlands at 5,000 metres where they set up their base camp.

I wrote to give our news. Five-year-old Michael had settled well into 'big' school, the fridge had stopped working, and a copy of the new Fairhead rock-climbing guidebook that we had jointly edited had just arrived in the post. I hoped my letters would make it through too, on their long trek in the other direction. They would probably arrive in twos or threes as the address I had for the expedition was a PO box in Kathmandu and the team had employed a mail-runner to deliver the post, at intervals, up to base camp.

I once asked Calvin if climbers ever wrote a letter – a final letter – to loved ones before setting off for a summit, a letter to be passed on only if the climber didn't return. He said that some did. I asked if he had ever written such a letter for me, but he said he hadn't. I wasn't sure how to feel about that.

Calvin's companions on the Makalu trip included some of Britain's most experienced and active alpinists, climbers he had got to know during his guide's training. They were all agreed, unequivocally, that the climbing style of the expedition would be the lightweight alpine approach. In mountaineering, a sport that has no rules, style is everything. Just getting to the top is never the whole story. How you climb – the level of difficulty and risk that you accept on a particular climb – is what determines your experience of it, physically, psychologically and emotionally. Your style also establishes your climbing credentials, to yourself and to other climbers. Over the years, improvements in training and equipment have made climbing easier and safer, but climbing styles have evolved in tandem with this so that each new generation can find its own levels of challenge.

There are two very different styles in Himalayan climbing: the traditional heavyweight system and the modern lightweight 'alpine' approach. Traditional expeditions lay siege to a mountain with an ever-rising network of support camps and fixed ropes until a couple of climbers can leave the top camp to embark on the final conquering push. It's usually sherpas or other high-altitude porters who set most of this extensive support system in place. They ferry loads to the high camps and kit them out with food, fuel and bottled oxygen. They 'fix' ropes – a skilled and sometimes dangerous job that involves anchoring the ropes to rock or ice to provide a sort of handrail and continuous supply line. Climbers can then clip to the ropes for security when they're going up or down. On steep sections they can attach handled clamps to the fixed ropes and haul themselves up.

Before the early 1990s, it was only 'real' climbers who ventured onto the big peaks, and nobody foresaw that this traditional siege system would be the basis for a whole new industry: the high-altitude tourism industry that would allow inexperienced clients to pay large sums to be shepherded in queues up those same fixed ropes and onto the highest summits.

In their lightweight approach, the Makalu team wouldn't be using bottled oxygen, and neither would they have sherpas working for them on the mountain. They considered it unethical to pay anyone to work in the risky environment above base camp. They felt very strongly too that any dependence on sherpas would undermine the integrity of their own climbing. Mountaineers like Reinhold Messner had shown that 8,000-metre peaks could be climbed in the same way as alpine ones 'by fair means', as he put it – without supplementary oxygen and without the additional support services of sherpas – as long as the climbers had the necessary fitness, skill and courage.

The Makalu climbers didn't plan to set up any fixed camps where food and equipment would be stockpiled in advance. When they headed off to climb, it would be as independent pairs carrying everything they needed for a multi-day ascent, just like in the Alps, except that these mountains were twice as high. They climbed some lower peaks in the area to acclimatise for Makalu and, inevitably, had to sit out some bad weather at base camp.

Now we were into October, and there were five weeks to go until the end of the expedition. Calvin's letters kept coming, and I kept writing too, with snippets of news big and small: it was reported on the radio that the Hungarian Socialists' Workers party had just disbanded itself – the Iron Curtain was wearing thin; the Department of Education inspector was due at my school and everyone was getting stressed; Michael had got croup and I'd had to call the doctor; 'Where's Daddy?' asked two-year-old Robert ten times a day. 'Is he climbing Makawu?' and there were days when the child wouldn't let me out of his sight; the baby, due in three months, was becoming quite a kicker – a good sign.

Of course I didn't have to mention to Calvin that I'd had to get the doctor for Michael. It could have waited and been part of the deluge of chat I'd share with him when he got home. But it would have taken a more generous-spirited spouse than me not to mention it. I found that there's nothing quite like worrying about a sick child in the middle of the night for igniting feelings of resentment against the missing parent. Michael got better, and I continued to mark off the days on the wall calendar.

The expedition had permits for five previously unclimbed faces and ridges on Makalu. Two of the group, Victor Saunders and Steve Sustad, succeeded in making the first ascent of the difficult west face of Makalu II and were very lucky to survive a storm on the descent.

Calvin, now well acclimatised, set out on Makalu with fellow mountain guide Rob Collister soon after this, but the storm had left the mountain in very poor condition. The slopes were covered with windslab, an avalanche-prone layer of unstable soft snow under a deceptive crust, and conditions didn't improve in the following weeks. By the time I got Calvin's letter detailing that attempt, winter had moved in on their base camp and they were already on their way home. At last.

Chapter 19

Oscar was born in January of 1990: a cheerful, lively baby who was much more vocal in his dislike of long car journeys and draughty tents than his brothers had been. We carried on with our climbing-centred lives anyway; the children were going to fit in with our plans rather than the other way around.

Oscar was six months old when we went to Chamonix that summer, and he still wasn't sleeping through the night. Snell's Field was long closed, and climbers now congregated at the campsite in the village of Argentière outside Chamonix. The tents were packed in close together, and at night I tried to shush him, anxious that he'd wake everyone as his wails sheared through the hundred tents around us. But he was having none of it. I tried giving him Dozol, but that didn't work. I tried giving him Southern Comfort (not much) mixed with warm water in his bottle – whose idea had that been? – but that didn't work either.

We yawned and sighed and took turns climbing. The only time we got undisturbed sleep was when we were bivouacking high in the mountains on the night before a climb. Whenever there was a good weather forecast, one or other of us would square our shoulders and go in search of a partner from among the Irish climbers in the campsite.

We were all working our way through the alpinists' bible, *The Mont Blanc Massif: The Hundred Finest Routes* by Gaston Rébuffat, and I was happy to find that Robbie Fenlon, a strong young Dublin-based alpinist like Donie, had ambitions for the same major route as me: the Walker Spur. Rébuffat rated it very highly and described it as 'a route to dream of, perhaps the finest in existence.' In terms of difficulty he placed it fourth from the top, at number ninety-seven, in his list of the finest hundred climbs. We checked the forecast again and packed our rucksacks. Calvin would be staying with the boys.

The Walker Spur is one of the six great north faces of the Alps. It is the magnificent buttress that had bewitched me when I looked across at it from the Moine bivy site back in 1974, its 1,200 metres of rock and snow rising darkly from the far side of the glacier. It sweeps up to the summit of the Grandes Jorasses, a mountain which at 4,208 metres forms the highest part of the formidable Jorasses ridge on the French–Italian frontier. We had our passports with us as we'd be descending into Italy.

The buttress lies at the far upper side of the Leschaux Glacier beyond the Mer de Glace, and it draws the eye of every climber and tourist who pauses at the Montenvers viewing point. Now, seventeen years since I'd first seen it, I didn't look up as we approached its base. I felt weak and unfit and had a dull ache in my lower back. We had been walking on the steepening glacier for over three hours, and my legs felt like lead as I struggled to keep up with Robbie. What was wrong with me? I mustn't have got back to my pre-baby fitness yet. Or was it that my period was due? Maybe it was just all the broken nights. 'Robbie, hang on,' I shouted. 'I'm wrecked. I don't think I can go on. I'll just slow you down too much.' Robbie waited till I caught up. 'If you wait here,' I panted, 'I'll go down and get Calvin, and you two can do the route together.'

Robbie very sensibly said no: the trip down to the valley and back up would take about eight hours. We stopped for a rest. He persuaded me that we should stick to our plan and bivouac on the upper reaches of the glacier, and then I could see how I felt in the morning. I felt fine in the morning – at least, as fine as you'd ever feel at 3 a.m. after a cold night on a thin foam mat on a sea of ice – especially when your period has just started.

It was still dark when we got moving. We made our way by

torchlight, roped and alert as we skirted crevasses and then found a way through the contorted ice of the huge *bergschrund*. At dawn we started up the buttress.

A day and a half later, we climbed onto the summit crest and looked down into Italy. We sat on our rucksacks in the snow and took a short rest as we viewed the descent. It had been a great route, and now it was a long way down to the Boccalatte Hut on the Italian side. Snow, ice, abseils over rock cliffs and then more snow . . . it was dark now, and still no sign of the hut. I was plodding in front, half asleep in the bouncing beam of my head torch, when my crampons scraped loudly on metal: I had walked onto the snowed-in roof of the Boccalatte Hut storeroom.

With tiredness suddenly flooding us, we circled down and around until we found the door to the main hut. It was dark and silent inside, but the guardian roused himself and brought us soup and cold beer. He was sorry there were no bed spaces left, but we didn't care as we sank onto the comfort of a wooden bench. At 2 a.m., a group of Italian climbers and their guides got up for an early start – they would be climbing up the slopes we had come down – and we slipped into their still-warm sleeping spaces.

The following morning we descended to the valley, hitched to the village of Courmayeur and got a bus back through the Mont Blanc tunnel to Chamonix.

'Ah, there you are!' said Calvin, giving me a hug. 'Well, how'd it go?'

'Great! What a route, and it's in good nick: very little stonefall. Robbie led the hardest pitch – the overhanging crack – but I got lots of good pitches too, like the 75-metre corner. It was handy enough, lots of bridging and well protected, but one of my leads in the Red Chimney – oh, scary! – stepping across some steep snow on a load of little stones that were just sticking out of the ice, and me in my rock shoes! Nasty! We bivied on top of the Grey Pillar. What about Oscar? Did he sleep?'

'No, not much.'

'You must be wrecked.'

'Yeah, but my gear's packed. I'll go while this weather holds.'

And within hours he was gone, to take his own turn on that great north face.

Back at home we continued our pattern of climbing whenever the weather was reasonable. We kept an obsessive eye on the forecast as the working week progressed, and by Thursday evening we'd make a decision on where to go: Fairhead, Donegal or the Burren in County Clare. It was always the Burren for the May bank-holiday weekend, and climbers from Dublin, Belfast, Cork and elsewhere would arrive to climb at the lovely sea cliff of Ailladie.

The sun usually shone, and there was a lively friendly atmosphere as everyone knew each other. Being part of that community of climbers, which now included a small number of active women, was a good motivator for Calvin and me. It made it easier for me to keep my focus in the days when continuing to climb while working and looking after three small children became exhausting.

It didn't help, of course, that our weekends away usually involved camping. Little ones dislike changes of routine, and being put down to sleep in a tent where the fabric just above your cot flaps away all night in an Atlantic breeze would be enough to upset any baby, as it did Oscar on the May bank holiday when he was one. We arrived late on the Friday night, and as soon as we opened the car doors the fresh sea air blasted in onto the three boys asleep in the back seat. The baby snuffled as we unpacked the camping stuff and whimpered as we tried to close the boot without making noise. In the beam of the headlights we pitched our two small tents on the carpet of short grass and springy sea pinks at the top of the cliff.

By the time we had brought the sleeping mats, sleeping bags, pillows, books, toys, clothes bags, bottles, baby food, nappy-change bag, cooking things, food box, stove, gas bottle and water bottle over to the tents, Michael and Robert had stumbled uncomplaining from the warm car, but Oscar was screaming his head off. A bottle for him and a nappy change and then we all settled down.

But not for long. Oscar was restless all through the night and still full of energy when the pitiless rays of the sun hit the tent at six in the morning. Once the other two had come over from their tent for breakfast, Oscar's empty travel cot was the only protected space when things got boisterous, and one or other of us would sometimes retreat into it. 'You go and climb first, love,' I offered. I was wondering how soon I could get Oscar back into the cot for a nap and be free to lie out on the smooth warm limestone pavement to stretch away the stiffness of a bad night. I'd have yesterday's *Irish Times* to hand and the silver espresso pot bubbling on the stove. But there was no answer from Calvin: he was curled up in the travel cot, snoring lightly.

Calvin guiding in the Mont Blanc Massif.

Photo: John Fox.

Below: With Robbie Fenlon at the ledge where we bivouacked on the Walker Spur.

Michael in Snell's Field, Chamonix.

Robert in the Italian Alps.

Oscar at Ailladie in the Burren, County Clare.

Camping at Ailladie.

High on the Bonatti Pillar. Me (top) reaching the belay above the huge shifting flake.

Sport climbing in Orpierre in the south of France. Bolts changed everything.

Calvin on the first ascent of Waist Deep in Alligators, Fairhead.

Me on Abyssinia – another new route at Fairhead.

Photo: Ricky Bell.

Chapter 20

'On top of the world' shouted the headline in the Sunday Tribune as it announced its coverage of the forthcoming Irish Manaslu Expedition in 1991. The article went on to say that the group of Irish mountaineers headed for Manaslu hoped to climb further and higher than any who had gone before them. Manaslu, 'Mountain of the Soul' was, it explained, one of the great peaks - 'the mountains exceeding 8,000 metres in height, and in all the world there are only 14 of them. None has been climbed by an Irish mountaineer.' And so the stage was set, and readers were promised regular articles that would cover the daring enterprise.

Manaslu is not a technically demanding mountain, but with a height of 8,163 metres it would give valuable high-altitude experience so the trip would serve as a dry run for the Everest expedition two years later. Calvin had been invited to join the team. The leader was Dawson Stelfox who had been with Ian Rea on Bhagirathi II in 1982 and who, like Ian, had built up a wealth of further experience in the intervening years. It was eleven strong, all male, and drawn from north and south. Even after twenty years of the Troubles, the border had no relevance for Irish mountaineers.

I didn't envy Calvin; expeditions are often tedious, sometimes dangerous and always long. I was happy to stay with the boys, who were now aged one, four and six. The coverage in the *Tribune* was to be by climber and writer Dermot Somers who would send back weekly reports. This was good. Well-written articles would help explain and legitimise our mountaineering world for extended family, sponsors, colleagues and anyone else with a passing interest.

So Sunday after Sunday I read of the beautiful Nepalese landscapes and the villages the climbers passed through on the walk-in, of life at base camp and of the effort it took to establish Camps 1 and 2, where the snow was deep and the air thin. But then came a report I had to read twice. It opened with some paragraphs in praise of Dawson's leadership qualities and then went on to give details of a disagreement that had arisen when a suggestion of Dawson's hadn't been accepted by everyone.

The disagreement concerned the climbing style of the expedition. In the planning stages, everyone had agreed that they would climb Manaslu in the best modern alpine style. But now that bad snow conditions had slowed things down, Dawson proposed that they change to the traditional siege approach. He wanted everyone to work together to stockpile food and equipment at high camps, to increase the chances of one pair making a successful summit bid. Success for them, after such a concerted effort, could then be taken as success for all, should no one else make it to the top. The newspaper article made particular mention of one 'vigorously contentious voice' that objected to the new strategy. I knew immediately that this must be Calvin. He would only ever climb alpine style, and he wouldn't hesitate to say so.

There's nothing unusual about arguments on expeditions, but if Dermot was treating the *Sunday Tribune* readership to an account of this one, a readership that was hardly well up on the subtleties of Himalayan climbing styles, I knew the row must be bad. The article concluded by stating confidently that Dawson's suggestion would be accepted by the group. I didn't think so, but I had to wait until Calvin came home to get the full story. He had been furious at the proposed change of plan. And he wasn't alone. Just four of the group were happy to accept it. For them, the lightweight alpine approach was just aspirational, whereas for Calvin and the other five it was a core doctrine.

The new plan would change everything. Working together to set up fixed camps would mean following a schedule. The climbers would have a rota for carrying loads, for sleeping at high camps, for recovering at base camp. Instead of climbing as independent pairs and operating according to their own fitness, ability and judgement, as Calvin had on all his previous expeditions, they'd have their movements regulated by a plan – someone else's plan.

Calvin would not, could not, accept any form of climbing in which he was not his own master and operating in the best style. And he wouldn't compromise his climbing style for anyone, not even on an 8,000-metre peak, not even to ensure a summit tick, for himself or for anyone else. Would I have been so clear myself that the style in which you climb is always more important than the summit to be bagged? I'm not sure. But what I am sure of is that Calvin's unswerving commitment to being the best climber he could possibly be, even in the face of strong arguments for expediency, was, and is, an essential part of his life force. And that force has energised both our lives.

There was no conclusion to the discussion in base camp. The group split, and both parties avoided speaking to each other for the rest of the trip. In the end, nobody got anywhere near the top of the mountain because of the constant heavy snowfall and the avalanche risk that came with it. It was an awkward split within such a small group, most of whom had been members of our little Dal Riada club, and it influenced the composition of the team for the first Irish attempt on Everest two years later. Calvin and the other rebels were left out of the reckoning, in spite of the letters of invitation that had been sent to them a few years before.

On that First Irish Everest Expedition in 1993, sherpa support, bottled oxygen, fixed ropes and fixed camps were all used. *Irish Times* journalist Lorna Siggins accompanied the expedition, and I sometimes skimmed through her newspaper articles, but I didn't feel any connection to the enterprise. Then, at eight o'clock one May morning, I was rooted to the kitchen floor by newsreader Anne Doyle's opening item on the RTÉ radio news: 'A thirty-seven-year-old Belfast architect has become the first Irish person to reach the summit of Mount Everest.' I felt a sharp stab of loss for what was gone forever now from Calvin's reach. It was a historic and demanding ascent. Dawson had climbed the last section of the north ridge to the summit on his own, his partner having turned back because of a malfunctioning oxygen set.

At school that day, the teacher who had sent away for the First Irish Everest Expedition educational poster was very excited. In the staffroom at break time colleagues asked me about weather windows and the death zone before turning to the real question of the day – whose turn was it to bring in the biscuits?

Calvin laughed whenever he heard himself described as having climbed Everest – it often happened – but he was never one to waste time on might-have-beens. Whatever the outcome of any trip, to mountains big or small, it was always the adventure of the next climb that fired his unquenchable exuberance.

Chapter 21

Throughout the 1990s, we continued to climb, with the three boys in tow. Easter holidays were spent at the limestone cliffs of Pembroke in South Wales, summers in Chamonix and countless spring and autumn weekends at Irish cliffs. Some of our climbing friends had children now too, and our boys had lots of wild, happy days in good company.

On one occasion at Fairhead it was just the five of us, and Calvin and I wanted to do a new route. We shepherded the boys, aged six, nine and eleven, down the Ballycastle Descent Gully and along the bottom of the cliff to where a huge boulder overhung a patch of flat ground. And there we left them, with a bag of treats, and rushed away to climb. This was still the pre-digital age, but we hoped they'd be able to amuse themselves, somehow, among the rocks.

The new route was a fair distance away, well out of sight, and we were gone for much longer than we intended. When we got back, hours later, the boys were understandably aggrieved, and we felt very guilty. To make it up to them, we said they could name the new climb. They decided to call it 'The X-Men', after their favourite superheroes. We didn't deserve such good children – not that day anyway.

Their weekends at home were normal. They'd go to gymnastics class, have friends around to play and choose a video to rent. If my father was babysitting he'd treat them to fast food and let them watch more television than I'd ever allow, and then read them some of the classics that he used to read to Bairbre and me.

For me, the really busy weekends were the ones when we stayed at home and 'did nothing'. That was when I'd catch up on the housework and do months of advance planning for my teaching and when Calvin and I would go to one of the new indoor climbing walls for a training session. The new walls were few and far between, but they were good, professionally designed training facilities, and they quickly became popular. Training on them was very sociable, and they were soon the focal points where climbers met up and maintained contact, replacing the midweek pub sessions that had been so central to traditional clubs. The indoor walls were invaluable to us over the winter months, and regular sessions on them became an important part of our climbing.

Friendly rivalry flourished at the climbing walls, and soon Calvin and others were making plans for a formal competition. The first Irish climbing competition was held in 1993, at an indoor climbing wall in Dublin City University. There were going to be separate climbs for men and women, and that surprised me as there were few enough men climbing harder on the crags than myself and my friend Joan Flanagan. It turned out that there was a lot to surprise me, not just about competitions but about how the whole nature of climbing was suddenly changing.

It was a bouldering competition, and each short 'problem' involved climbing up a series of marked holds on the indoor climbing wall and then jumping back down onto crash mats. The problems were short and fierce and required power. Good footwork, balance and stamina, my fortes, were of little use, and the shifting audience of waiting climbers made me nervous. There were far more competitors than I had expected, and I didn't recognise most of them. A slight girl called Siobhán sailed up the problems I was falling off. She seemed to have fingers of steel. Where had she come from?

In the end, I got third place, behind her and Joan. There was worse to come. I had turned forty the previous summer, and when the prize-giving was coming to an end in the college bar, my name was called again. 'And now, the Female Veteran Prize goes to . . . Clare Sheridan!'

Veteran? With a grinding smile I weathered the applause and accepted my prize before subjecting Calvin to a muttered barrage of questions. 'What was that all about? Whose idea was that? So embarrassing!'

'Jack just wanted to present you –'

'Yeah, but how did he know I was forty? You told him, you must have.'

'Well, he asked.'

We were all tired and hungry on the way home in the car, but I couldn't let it go. 'You told him I was forty! God!'

'But you've never lied about your age. You've never minded people knowing your age.'

'Yeah, but that doesn't mean I want it shouted from the rooftops, especially since they're all so . . . *young*, all those students, and I'm only just forty!'

I expected one of the boys in the back seat to correct me and say I was actually forty and a half. They had made me a big four-oh birthday card in Chamonix the previous summer, with a little cartoon figure on top of a snowy peak. Michael had written CLARE on the front (they always used our first names rather than 'Mum' and 'Dad') and had decorated it with big soft blobs of snow. For them, forty was just the number after thirty-nine. I frowned into the rear-view mirror. The toddler was asleep, and the other two were each staring out their own side window, distancing themselves from the heat in the front. OK, time to shut up.

We were in the Alps the following summer and when the weather became cool and unsettled in the middle of August, you could hear the cowbells in the clear air as the campsite emptied. Other families with climbing fathers – friends from Ireland and Scotland – packed up their tents and headed home. Our boys were bereft as they watched them leave and would happily have gone home too, but Calvin and I weren't ready to let autumn catch up on us just yet. We decided to drive south to try out the new 'sport climbing' crags that everyone was talking about.

The south of France was like a different continent for the boys. They stared at the bulging yellow and orange gourds piled high at the roadside farm stalls and jumped in surprise when lizards darted past their sandals. It was warm even after dark, and the night air was full of the rhythmic ticking of insects. The new campsite had a playground, a swimming pool and a café-bar, and the limestone cliffs were just a short walk away. This was beginning to feel like a holiday in a way that our time in Chamonix, with its serious and committing climbs and threatening storms, never did.

The cliffs were equipped with bolts, line after glinting line of them. Holes had been drilled into the rock at regular intervals and steel expansion bolts fixed securely into them. The head of each bolt had an eye to which a karabiner could be clipped by a passing climber as a connection point for their rope. With a bolt to clip every few metres, you could staple your rope to the rock and eliminate any risk of a sizeable fall.

Traditional protection pieces are always removed by the second climber as they ascend, but bolts modify the rock permanently as the metal is left in place indefinitely. Bolts are particularly useful on sections of compact rock where there are no cracks for jamming in traditional protection gear. Walls that had looked surreally steep and blank to previous generations were now climbable.

When bolts began to proliferate on the Continent in the 1980s, they gave rise to huge controversy because their use challenged what had been understood to be the essential nature of climbing: the management of risk while engaging in a physically demanding sporting activity. The head game of staying cool as you managed that risk had been one of the core elements of climbing since its earliest days, but now people could rock climb in almost complete safety and concentrate simply on the physical difficulties. Reinhold Messner called it 'the murder of the impossible'.

We saw whole families coming to the crags with their dogs and their picnics, and there were suddenly a lot of women leading. The old dictum – *the leader never falls* – wasn't relevant in sport climbing. Now it was safe to fall because you were virtually guaranteed not to hurt yourself as you'd never drop very far. People took falls regularly and casually, sometimes even letting go deliberately to save their strength. They would then rest and puzzle out the next few moves while dangling safely below a bolt.

Even middle-grade climbers now aspired to higher and higher technical grades, practising until they achieved mastery. They top-roped – when attempting a hard climb they opted for having the complete security of a rope from above instead of risking the challenge of leading the climb. This made sense if you saw climbing as a series of moves to be perfected but to Calvin and me it seemed a shameful cop-out, a turning away from the true spirit of climbing. Calvin called it a bastard practice.

Climbing up a rock face or a mountain and solving its puzzles as you found them, without prior familiarity or the security of preplaced hardware, was the basis of all serious mountaineering, but now this approach had come to be seen as just another style of climbing. It was labelled traditional or 'trad' and continued to attract just a few devotees, while the number of bolt-clipping *sport* climbers boomed. Most of these new climbers never looked to the mountains. They concentrated instead on the technical difficulty of a single rope length of rock and the grade was the most important aspect of it. Climbing for them involved a quantifiable athletic effort within a managed environment and as such it had more in common with many other sports than it had with the complex, multifaceted and unpredictable activity that Calvin and I had been introduced to in the 1960s and 1970s.

Trad climbing had only ever appealed to a small number of women, mainly because of the risk involved, but sport climbing quickly became popular with both sexes. The gym-like atmosphere of indoor walls was perfect for finessing technique and building power, and training helped narrow the gap between men's and women's climbing standards. Young women and girls developed strength that amazed me, and they did this with the honed muscles of gymnasts and not, as I had once feared, the bulging physiques of bodybuilders. But even with their new strength few were tempted onto non-bolted crags.

Standards soared as training became more sophisticated. Top sport climbers were sponsored by gear companies and became performers.

They would train intensively on their 'project' for weeks, months, or even years, sometimes recreating a particular sequence of holds, at a particular angle of steepness, on an indoor wall until, through endless rehearsal, they had perfected their movements. Then they would climb it in one go while a professional photographer or film-maker recorded the feat. Climbing magazines had pictures of them pulling up bulging rock using just two fingers stuck into tiny holes, or moving like geckos under big horizontal roofs as they displayed levels of skill and athleticism that would have been undreamt of just a few years before.

Compared to the raw crucible of the Alps, the sport-climbing venue we had moved to in Provence was a relaxed playground, a sunny arena with an inviting choice of prepared test pieces. We found the steepness of the sport climbs exhilarating but physically demanding. It soon showed up my lack of power, and we both fought tooth and nail not to fall off – old habits die hard.

We were having fun, but the boys got tired of waiting around for us. We were at a crag one day when the younger two became bored and restless. They had been sitting all morning in a shifting patch of shade below the rock face and had finished off their biscuits and swapped their comics. I was hoping we'd get another short route done before there was outright rebellion, and then I overheard Michael, who was thirteen, quietly pass on some advice to Robert and Oscar. 'Just let them play,' he counselled, 'and get it over with.'

Little wonder, I suppose, that they never became enthusiastic about climbing themselves. This didn't bother Calvin or me – climbing either grabs you or it doesn't and, though many of our friends and acquaintances had children who liked to climb, very few of those youngsters maintained an interest in it beyond their teens. It was much more important to us that our boys should grow up with an awareness of what the outdoors has to offer and that they'd understand how wild places can bring balm to both body and soul.

From then on we always took time to visit the bolted crags in the south of France as our Continental summers were coming to a close. Sport climbing was enjoyably stress-free, and the featureless, smooth rock faces with their sequences of small holds were as close to indoor climbing walls as you could get. We never 'worked' routes the way serious sport climbers did, and when pre-practice also became acceptable on hard trad routes, we stayed with the style we'd always used: the *onsight* style of doing a climb in one go without pre-practice and without resting on gear. As the most psychologically demanding type of climbing, it was still, for us, the most rewarding.

Chapter 22

Calvin and I did a lot of voluntary work for the FMCI. We edited rock-climbing guidebooks and annual new-climbs bulletins, wrote alpine reports and other articles for the FMCI journal *Mountain Log*, sat on various committees and took on roles such as lectures officer. When I was lectures officer in 1995, I decided to invite British alpinist Alison Hargreaves to give a slideshow in Dublin.

I had met Alison back in 1983 at a women's climbing meet in North Wales. I knew a little about her already because she had been featured in one of the British climbing magazines as an up-and-coming young rock climber, and I was interested to meet her. I was interested to meet everyone who came along that weekend because it was my first experience of being in the company of serious women climbers. There was some interest in me too because of the new routes I was doing at Fairhead. Apparently women doing first ascents were pretty rare in Britain.

There was some confusion at first between Clare Torrans and Clare Sheridan. This was a few years after we had got married, and I was using Calvin's surname at the time. When we came back to Ireland in 1982 after our year in America, I was anxious to melt back into the teaching profession as an unremarked-on married woman. Being 'Mrs Torrans' was useful for that. This was the country, after all, where High Court judge Rory O'Hanlon could state in a famous court case in the early 1980s that sexual relations outside marriage constituted 'a violation of bodily integrity'. I switched back to 'Ms Sheridan' in the early 1990s because, while divorce wasn't legalised until 1996, I was living and working happily in Bray – a somewhat liberal enclave at the outer reaches of the capital – and 'Mrs' had never sat well with me.

The women's meet in 1983 was hosted by the Pinnacle Club, an all-women's climbing club which had as its hut a little stone cottage below Snowdon. I loved the atmosphere in the hut as people arrived in twos and threes and excited female voices chattered away about climbing.

Alison was easy to spot, all bouncing curls and spiky ambition. At twenty-one she was one of the youngest there, and she spoke, just a little too loudly, about all the climbs she had done and all the climbs she intended to do. By chance, she and I ended up climbing side by side on parallel cracks the following day, on the sea cliff at Gogarth, near Holyhead.

By the early 1980s, the grading system for classifying the difficulty of climbs had become more sophisticated. Instead of the open-ended XS or Extremely Severe as the top grade, 'Extreme' was now broken down into E1, E2, E3, etc. That day on Gogarth Alison climbed 'Park Lane', an E1, while I tackled the neighbouring crack, 'The Strand', an E2. Going by the routes she said she had done, I reckoned we were both climbing at about the same standard – E3 on a good day and with ambitions for E4. The small group of top British, American and French female climbers who now appeared regularly in the climbing magazines were already climbing E4 and E5 and eyeing up the E6s.

I didn't kid myself that I'd ever be an equal among that elite group, but over the two days of the meet I could feel the exciting dynamic that emerges when strong women climb together. I'd had a couple of opportunities to climb with women before that weekend, and I'd found that it was a different experience from climbing with men. The support that women give each other is warmer and more encouraging than that given by men. And women actually admit it if they're scared on a climb while men don't. I realised that climbing in the company of strong women would probably revolutionise my own mental approach, but there were never enough women active on the Irish cliffs to provide that sort of psychological springboard. It's only now, almost four decades after that meet in Wales, that I'm no longer surprised if I see a woman leading an Extreme climb in the Burren, Donegal or Fairhead.

Alison didn't join the top women rock climbers either and soon turned her attention to alpine and then Himalayan climbing. She found that, unlike most women or indeed men, she had the physical and mental strength needed for difficult climbs in big mountains. Her ascents got good coverage in the British climbing magazines, and the same magazines that had ignored women for so long suddenly had lots of photographs of them.

When Alison climbed the notorious North Face of the Eiger in the summer of 1988, she was the first British woman to do so. That fact alone made her ascent very noteworthy, but she was also, at the time, five and a half months pregnant with her first child. She was intent on making a name for herself as a climber, but to do a route like that while pregnant? I admired her achievement but thought that, overall, the ascent had the air of a stunt about it and I wondered why she was trying so hard.

At the time I didn't appreciate that Alison wanted to make a career out of climbing and was anxious to get any media coverage she could. In 1993, she undertook an alpine challenge that was guaranteed to grab the headlines: she would climb the six great north faces of the Alps, but she would do it solo and over just one summer. It was a very formidable undertaking. She now had two children, and her husband, also a climber, spurred her on and minded the children in damp tents all over the Alps of Switzerland, Italy and France as she carried out her plan.

She succeeded in soloing the six north faces and in the autumn wrote a book about her experience: *A Hard Day's Summer*. But did she really climb the north faces? On some of them she didn't actually climb the established classic lines but followed easier or shorter variations. Climbers were very critical of this, and the suggestion of fraud hung over the whole endeavour. It had been a major miscalculation on Alison's part not to climb the exact historic lines and it undermined her achievement, but the climbing she did do went far beyond what any British woman had ever done in the Alps before. And she did it solo.

I had great admiration for Alison's mental toughness, her ability to climb thousands of metres of steep rock, snow and ice, sometimes in unsettled weather, and with no one to share the stress. Variations or not, I wanted to hear her story. I didn't know any men, much less women, who had done anything like that.

In 1995, Alison was training hard for an attempt on Everest. She intended to climb it solo and without bottled oxygen. When she came to Ireland to give her lecture, she stayed with us in Bray. She was a different person now from the young woman I'd met twelve years earlier. She was mature and thoughtful, and I was very interested to hear how she fitted her intensive training programme in around caring for her children. The date of her lecture happened to be the first of February – the feast of St Brigid, one of the patron saints of Ireland, or, if you go back far enough, a pagan goddess – and when I was introducing her I suggested that this made it a suitable date for her talk.

Three months later, in May 1995, Alison climbed Everest without bottled oxygen, and she did it solo – totally unsupported by sherpas or teammates. She was only the second person ever to reach the summit in such a challenging style (the first being Reinhold Messner) and it was an extraordinary achievement. She was fêted in the press. 'One of the greatest climbs in history,' said the front-page headline in *The Times*. The fact that this exceptional Himalayan climber was not just a woman but also a mother added to the fascination.

There were dissenting voices, however. Nigella Lawson, also in *The Times*, made the comment that Alison's mountaineering showed 'a reality-denying self-centredness'. Alison was confounded by this, but reeling already from the media interest in her ascent of Everest, she had no time to collect her wits before she was off to climb K2 a few weeks later.

We were in Chamonix as usual that summer, and I was having a shower at the campsite when I heard Michael arrive panting at the door of the cubicle. 'Clare, Clare,' he said, in the urgent tones of a child who knows he has real news, 'Alison Hargreaves is dead! She was killed on K2!' My first thought was to quieten him down – it wasn't seemly somehow. But then that wasn't important. He remembered her, of course. It was only months since she had stayed with us, and we'd never had a visiting female climber as a guest before. And then I took it in. Alison, the brave, had been blown to her death off K2.

The initial shocked headlines that went around the world were followed, almost immediately, by a swelling tide of vilification. I read the various articles with fascination and disquiet. They all seemed to be asking the same thing: what right had she to be climbing dangerous peaks? 'An unfit mother,' cried the *Guardian*, and there was discussion about what age children might be before a mother could consider 'leaving' them. There was no discussion about the fathers who had died climbing in the Himalayas that summer. In the *Guardian*, Polly Toynbee wrote about danger being powerfully addictive, like crack, and left an image in the public mind of Alison as a person who craved risk just for the sake of it and who in so doing had 'behaved like a man'. This last revealing comment aside, Toynbee's criticism was way off the mark.

The young woman I had got to know was a committed parent who was trying to carve out a career for herself in the only way she knew how: by climbing hard mountains. In *Regions of the Heart*, a sympathetic and compelling biography of Alison that was published on the fourth anniversary of her death, authors David Rose and Ed Douglas reveal the emotional turbulence that lay behind her ambitious sports plan for that fateful year. She was under a lot of pressure both personally and financially and had hoped that by climbing K2 as well as Everest she would ensure an income for herself and her children, through sponsorship, lectures and a book deal. But she wasn't on K2 just to guarantee an income. She was there because she knew she could climb it, well-armed as she was with her great experience, courage and skill. The opportunity to test herself on such a formidable peak fired her up, even as she ached to get back to her ordinary life with her children.

Poor Alison. I was shocked by her death and very sorry for her children who were aged just four and six at the time. I dismissed the critical press coverage as disrespectful to her and irrelevant to me. I felt that the general public had so little understanding of climbing and of the motivations of climbers, of either gender, that such criticism was sexist and didn't deserve consideration.

Alison's high-level mountaineering was indeed risky, but she worked very hard to manage that risk and never chose to be reckless. She was accused of being selfish, but she was only selfish to the extent that anyone, male or female, is selfish if they give time to an activity that they engage in for themselves alone, an activity that makes them feel strong in body and spirit and fills them with exhilaration. She acted like a man? Yes. Because for far too long the choice of being selfish like that has only been open to men.

Chapter 23

We never went on holiday. The two months we spent in the Alps every summer were all about climbing. They never involved sunbathing or dining out or indulging in expensive treats like the Cornettos they sold at the campsite office. Those were for the children who came for just two weeks – the children who were on holiday. But you could get a packet of eight Cornettos in the *hypermarché* down the valley for the price of one at the campsite. 'Eat them before they melt!' I'd order as I handed two ice creams in quick succession to each of the boys as we stood in the shimmering heat of the supermarket car park.

When the weather was good, the campsite in Argentière was idyllic. We took turns climbing and our boys joined other kids to range unchecked through the nearby forests, constructing huts and burying treasure. But the weather was often unsettled, and when it rained our lives contracted to the four stretched cotton walls of our tent. We had a chalet-style tent now, one you could stand up in, but it didn't keep the water out during heavy downpours. The campsite would become an expanse of sagging tents and muddy paths, with straggles of mist catching in the surrounding pine trees.

The ground was sloped, and there would soon be a treacherous little stream seeking out the dimples in the groundsheet. The boys would rush to move their toys and comics to the safety of the car while I piled the clothes and bedding onto the island of waterproof sleeping mats in the middle of the floor. Then Calvin would pull on his rain jacket and head out into the deluge to dig a trench around the tent with his ice axe. As the water gurgled through the new channels, he'd stand back and admire it: 'Now that's a bit more Protestant-looking!'

Then we'd hunker down, the boys zooming around in the tent with their Batmobile and action figures, me back in my sleeping bag and deep in a book, and Calvin sitting cross-legged on his mat, a pile of guidebooks fanned out in front of him. He spent a few weeks every summer working as an alpine guide, and he was always meticulous in his preparations. This wasn't easy in a small crowded space shared with four other people. He'd triple-check everything that he might need for himself and his clients as he waited for the weather to clear. Then he'd bring the clients high above the snow line for some of the most memorable days of their lives, and by the time he'd deliver them back to the valley he'd be mentally and physically drained. After that he could relax and just have the boys to worry about while I took my chance to leave for a climb.

On the morning I was setting off for the Bonatti Pillar, he slept on. I was hoping he'd wake up and wish me luck. It was 7 a.m., and the grass outside the tent was heavy with dew. I checked my rucksack again – rock shoes, harness, rope, helmet, ice axe – all the obvious things were there. I was ready to leave, but just as I was about to swing my rucksack up onto my shoulders, I heard a child's voice. 'Clare, I can't remember what your face looks like.'

I stopped dead. The voice, from inside the tent, was Oscar's. It came again, more insistent this time. 'Clare, wait, I can't –'

'Shh, you'll wake the others.' I unzipped the tent as quietly as I could and then the flimsy inner door to where the boys were sleeping. Two bright accusing eyes looked up at me from the jumble of sleeping bags. Oscar, aged six, was wide awake. 'Shh! Don't wake the others! Look, here I am, and I'll be back soon. Bye.' He said nothing, and I left. I felt sick. This would definitely be the last. The last *Grande Course*, the last big alpine classic that I would be thrilled to have done but that I found harder and harder to commit to with every passing summer.

The *Grandes Courses* were the great climbs that were forged by the alpine superheroes of the 1940s and 1950s. The actual climbing was easier now because modern climbers had better footwear and lighter equipment, but the objective dangers – the random risks that you had no control over – were as threatening as ever. Avalanches, storms, rockfall, this was where luck came in, whatever your experience or ability. And the climb I was heading for seemed to have more than its share of objective dangers. On the approach we'd be avoiding crevasses and collapsing ice walls as we crossed a high glacier. Then, to get to the base of the climb, we would do multiple abseils into a couloir that was battered by stonefall. The climb itself, almost 700 metres of steep rock, would be hard to retreat from if a storm broke. A summer storm would bring torrential rain, or snow, and thunder and lightning. Every climber's dread is the sound of the metal climbing gear humming just before a lightning strike. I'd never been hit, but the tales I'd heard from those who had were terrifying.

Was it worth it?

When our boys were infants and toddlers I would head off to do big climbs without a backward glance, happy they were in safe hands and knowing I'd appreciate them even more when I got back, exhausted but fizzing with joy. Now that I was older, the great alpine challenges seemed less worth the candle. But there was one climb that I longed to do: the Bonatti Pillar.

On my first visit to Chamonix in 1974, I had noticed a very striking picture in the window of a photographic shop. It was a magnificent black-and-white shot of the slender peak known as the Petit Dru. The tapering face of the mountain was lit by an ethereal light, and from the snow-dusted ledges at its base the sharp-edged ridges rose and gleamed against a dark sky. This elegant spire dominated the skyline beyond Snell's Field. After rain it would sometimes emerge above the clouds, a sunlit sentinel shining over the dank murk of the valley. You couldn't see it without wanting to climb it. On the right-hand flank of the mountain, the huge buttress of the Bonatti Pillar soared up from a shadowy couloir. It was one of the most famous and most beautiful alpine climbs in the world.

That first alpine summer, I had stopped to look at the photograph every time I passed the shop, wondering each time if I should buy it. It was expensive, and my funds were very limited, but on the last day I decided I couldn't go home without it. It came in a thin white paper bag and I carried it in my hand all the way home rather than risk getting it squashed inside my rucksack. I slept on the floor of Le Bourget Airport en route and woke to find that the bag was gone. I spotted it just in time - sticking out of a bin with a cleaner about to empty a dustpan on top of it. When I got back to my parents' house, I put it up on the wall in the room I still shared with Bairbre. It had been on the wall of every house I'd lived in for the twenty-two years since then.

And now, in 1996, I had a chance to climb the Dru, by the Bonatti Pillar, and it was time to leave. I hoped Oscar had gone back to sleep. Malcolm, my half-English half-French climbing partner, would be waiting for me at the Montenvers mountain railway station in Chamonix. He had just turned eighteen, and he'd have enough enthusiasm for both of us.

The following morning, after a bivouac on the airy Flammes de Pierre ridge, we abseiled into the rocky depths of the Dru couloir and pulled our ropes down from the last anchor. Now we were committed. We were level with the start of our climb and only the steep funnel of the gully lay in between. It was 40 or 50 metres across, and its sloped surface was pitted from the impact of falling rocks. We'd heard the sudden whoosh of stones cutting the air and then the cracks and thuds of nearby hits. We stood and listened.

The previous year, Calvin and I had got to know a young American climber in the Argentière campsite. He had gone to climb the Bonatti Pillar but had died in this couloir in an abseiling accident. His camper van stayed parked below our tent for a week until the gendarmes came to tow it away.

We listened again. Nothing. Malcolm belayed me, and I ran the gauntlet of the couloir to reach the ledge at the base of the pillar. There was still no sound, and he followed. Now that we were ready to start the climb, it began to feel right at last. We swung leads (taking turns to lead every second pitch), made good progress up cracks and onto ledges and went astray the odd time as dozens of others must have gone astray before us.

It was my lead. I came to the foot of a big flake of rock that had a crack running all the way around it, detaching it from the main face. It was like a huge door that was slightly ajar. I stood on tiptoe to put some gear into the crack and, once clipped, began to layback up the side of it. Laybacking is both strenuous and delicate. It involves hanging from the side of a crack, in the shape of the letter C, your arms horizontal as you pull on the crack's edge and your feet more or less horizontal too as you walk them up the rock towards your hands. As you move each hand and foot in turn you have to take care not to upset the balance between pulling and pushing – the tension that's holding you suspended in place. Taking a hand off to put in gear is tricky, but I was well above my protection now and had to get something else in. I sized up the crack but just as I reached to unclip gear from my harness, the world jolted as the whole multi-ton slice of rock suddenly shifted. I squawked with fright. The granite door had opened further, and I was hanging from the side of it. I froze, waiting for it to detach from the face and plummet to the glacier hundreds of metres below.

But it didn't. It had jammed into its new position, for the moment. Would it stay put? I was more than halfway up it so it might be safer to go on. Would I be lighter if I held my breath? I couldn't work that out. 'I'll have to go on,' I shouted down to Malcolm, who was looking up in alarm. He was directly in the line of fire.

'Be careful,' he replied. Be careful? How the hell could I be careful? I couldn't even put any gear in to clip to as wedging something into the widening crack might dislodge the flake completely. I climbed on up as smoothly as I could and anchored myself, shaking, to the solid rock face above.

That night we slept on a ledge two-thirds of the way up the pillar, and when we woke at dawn we could see lightning flashing inside dark clouds in the distance. We packed up quickly and didn't pause to light the stove to make tea. Getting off the lightning-attracting pillar was our priority now, not breakfast. We climbed the remaining pitches at top speed and began the descent. The sky had cleared by then, and we were able to relax a little though we didn't let our concentration slip for even a moment – most accidents happen on the descent.

Back at the bivy site on the Flammes de Pierre ridge, other climbers had arrived, hoping to do the route the following day. They had been watching our progress, and when we climbed down onto the big bivy ledge, one of them applauded and handed us mugs of strong sweet coffee. It was renowned alpinist Ivan Ghirardini. To him we must have looked like a mother and son: I was forty-four and Malcolm still a gangly teenager.

Down in the valley Calvin had everything packed up ready for the drive home. The end of another alpine season. *Got away with it again*, I thought. But I wouldn't push my luck. From then on I was more conservative in my choice of route, but there is no such thing as a worthwhile alpine climb that is free of objective dangers.

Over the next few years there was a lot of rockfall on the Petit Dru until finally, in 2005, much of the Bonatti Pillar collapsed in a series of thunderous crashes and monstrous clouds of dust.

Chapter 24

Ian Rea and Eddie Cooper were Calvin's closest climbing friends. They were also mountaineers for whom he had the greatest respect. He'd shared many intense days with them on rock, snow and ice over the twenty-five years since the Shivling expedition. In Alaska in 1996 they climbed Mount Foraker via the remote and rarely travelled Sultana Ridge and then the West Rib of Denali (Mount McKinley), North America's pre-eminent peak. Both routes were first Irish ascents but then almost all of their big climbs were, whether in the Alps or in the greater ranges.

When they came home from Alaska they started planning for K2. This spectacular pyramid was the most difficult of the 8,000-metre peaks and, at 8,611 metres, the second-highest in the world. It had never been attempted by an Irish party. The expedition was scheduled for the summer of 1998. Calvin was fifty-five, and this would be his ninth expedition.

The team of six was a very strong one, and the expedition got some good publicity in the months before they left. Calvin did interviews on RTÉ radio, and when the *Irish Times* published a photograph of him abseiling from the roof of the Gresham Hotel, in Dublin, my father had a copy of it framed. The climbers met Taoiseach Bertie Ahern and were invited to Áras an Uachtaráin where President Mary McAleese compared notes with Calvin on the streets they'd grown up in in Belfast – just a stone's throw from each other, but social and tribal worlds apart.

Whenever Calvin was going away on an expedition, I was always annoyed with myself if I got upset saying goodbye. Getting emotional was such a weak, pointless, *womany* thing. When I was the one to take off – to climb frozen waterfalls in the Alps during the February midterm or to search out good snow and ice conditions in Scotland if it was an early Easter – he would always wave me off without hesitation. For him climbing was so life-affirming that the negatives never got a look-in. And what right had I to show worry? I'd left enough people standing and waving over the years. 'Be careful,' my mother would say as she gave me her quick get-it-over-with hug. 'Tao,' my father would smile – my old pet name – and fold me into his big bear hug.

When he was in his eighties, my father developed cancer and was unlucky enough to contract a deadly hospital bug while being treated in Loughlinstown, the local hospital. In the space of a month he went from being well enough to hill walk with retired friends to being in need of palliative care in the same hospital. Two days before he died, the nurses wheeled his bed out of the busy ward and into a small side room. The seven of us, his children, took turns to sit with him, bringing my mother along for as much as she could take.

On the second-last day, I went to the hospital after school to relieve my brother Shane. My father was unconscious at this stage. I sat for a while listening to his laboured breathing before leaning close to say sorry: sorry for all those times I'd shouldered my rucksack and walked away to the mountains, oblivious to the tide of worry I was leaving in my wake.

I could never object to Calvin going away on big climbing trips. I knew how important it was for him to play that game, to test his skill and courage in the unpredictable arena of the high mountains. Asking him not to go would have been like denying a very fine pianist access to a piano. But I hated the prospect of spending months without him – my lover, my friend, my climbing partner whose spirit never faltered.

When the morning for Calvin's departure came, we had to be at the airport at 6 a.m. We all milled around, the warriors and the wives, waiting for the time to run out. It was definitely more fun to be a warrior than a wife. Ian's wife, Moira, had come to see him off. A climber herself, she was now expecting their first child. The others – Eddie Cooper, Donie O'Sullivan, Martin Daly and Paul Dunlop – had already said goodbye to loved ones at home. I stood by with our three boys as Calvin checked his documents. I reminded him to send postcards to family and friends and to buy spare batteries for his Walkman. I didn't tell him to be careful – I knew he'd never be reckless.

There was still time left before the flight, but then the heart-fraying tension was broken when the cheerful figure of Harry O'Brien came bounding in. Harry had been a member of the Spillikin Club and then Dal Riada, and had been with us on the Andean expedition in 1980. He had also been a member of the controversy-mired Manaslu trip where he had remained staunchly committed to the lightweight alpine-style approach. Now he and his wife Ann had come with champagne to wish success to this latest alpine-style Himalayan endeavour. We just had time to toast the travellers when the flight was called. The last hug. 'Mind yourself,' I heard myself saying, but I didn't have time to get upset.

The route to the K2 base camp was via the stunning Concordia glacier in the heart of Pakistan's Karakoram range. This giants' playground, the junction of five huge ice flows, lies low between some of the highest summits in the world. They eclipse each other's bulk as they crowd the skyline, but one peak stands in isolation. This is the mighty cone of K2. Calvin told me that they had to force themselves not to look away when its intimidating splendour first came into view.

This group were all committed to climbing K2 the hard way: they wouldn't be using artificial oxygen, high-altitude porters or sherpas, fixed camps or fixed ropes. More fool them, some people thought. Wasn't K2, the killer mountain, challenging enough? No fixed ropes? What about ropes fixed by other expeditions on the same route? No, repeated Calvin, they wouldn't be using them either, but if things went wrong they'd use any fixed ropes they came across to try and get down in one piece. They wouldn't die for their ideals. That sounded reassuring, to an extent.

Back in Ireland I sat at the computer, frustrated and anxious. I'd never sent an email before. I was at a friend's house, and it took us two hours to work out how to get the message typed and sent. It seemed a technological miracle to be able to email base camp, but I just couldn't get the words to say what I wanted. The expedition had a satellite phone, but I didn't see it as much of an asset, unless there was an emergency. Calvin rarely used it, but every time I left the house I was afraid I was going to miss a call from him. I dug out his musty old fleece, the one with the broken zip that he'd left behind in the bottom of the wardrobe, and buried my face in it. The house was strangely empty as fourteen-year-old Michael was away too, on a Gaeltacht course in the Aran Islands.

Calvin's letters kept coming, with an extra page of notes and sketches for the boys. My own letters rambled: I'd pulled a muscle and was so bored, not being able to run or climb, that I'd painted the utility room; the Tour de France had come to Ireland and we had walked to the top of the road near our estate to watch it flash by; trouble had flared up in the North again, and no one was crossing the border unless they had to; Michael wasn't impressed with the Gaeltacht and had listed his complaints to me over the phone – they included obligatory Irish dancing in the open, even in gale-force winds.

Broad Peak, a less demanding undertaking than K2, was to be the team's first objective, and they all hoped to acclimatise on it. Eddie Cooper stormed up it, master of his chosen style, and made it to the fore summit at 8,034 metres, despite having damaged his ribs in a fall. The others didn't fare as well. They all climbed to well over 7,000 metres, but then incipient frostbite, bad weather and altitude sickness – the usual hazards of high-altitude climbing – beat them back.

Calvin was making a second attempt when he was hit by a falling rock. He was concussed, and though he was able to make his way back down off the mountain, he suffered from headaches and neck pains for days afterwards. I read about his accident in an emailed expedition report, but before I had time to get worried he rang on the satellite phone to say that he was fine.

He wasn't fine actually, and when the team moved over to K2 he continued to have pains in his head and neck. He climbed up to Camp 1 but didn't attempt to go any higher. There were climbers from four other countries attempting K2 that summer, all using the siege fixed-rope approach, but even they had no success because of the very poor weather conditions. Eddie and Paul struggled to a point above Camp 2 before turning back, and no one made it as far as Camp 3 that year. But the Irish climbers came home in good spirits, happy that Eddie's fine achievement in climbing to over 8,000 metres on Broad Peak, in alpine style, showed what Irish climbers were capable of.

The new millennium brought a major change in the world of Himalayan climbing. The number of people engaging in high-altitude mountaineering increased dramatically as more and more individuals came to see it as a type of adventure tourism. Guiding companies proliferated and sought to woo non-climbers as would-be consumers and within a decade Everest had been reduced to the status of a bucket-list item.

The majority of the newcomers were fit and determined, and had ready cash, but lacked the experience and ability to climb independently. Many of them referred to themselves as adventurers rather than mountaineers, and they signed up to join multinational groups on commercially organised ascents where the services provided – mountain-guide support, sherpa support, bottled oxygen, fixed ropes and pre-equipped camps – made up for their lack of expertise. For those who could afford luxury on the mountain, there were tents with heat and furnishings at some of the high camps, the equipment having been carried up by sherpas before the start of the busy climbing season. The fixed ropes multiplied, as did the number of people clamped to them, and in time even K2 became somewhat tamed and packaged.

Chapter 25

The K2 trip was Calvin's last big expedition. This wasn't due to any decision on his part but it just worked out that way. By the mid 2000s he was in his sixties and I into my fifties but we never stopped climbing. Regular training on indoor walls helped us maintain a good standard, and as the boys were now old enough to look after themselves we were free to go on climbing trips together again. We spent days and nights on spectacularly beautiful mountains in the Alps and further afield but were always drawn back to Fairhead on the north Antrim coast.

Climbing at Fairhead doesn't feel like sport – it feels like spending time in another realm. You stand dwarfed below its palisade of pillars, buttresses and walls while you uncoil your ropes and tighten your rock shoes. The talk between you and your partner is scant – this isn't the time for conversation.

Then you check your knot, step off the grass and commit to the steepness. Immediately the rock absorbs you, filling your vision and curving round to enclose you as you climb. After a hundred vertical metres your fingers curl over the square-cut cliff edge and you pull up from the monochrome into the sunlight. The moorland, lakes and farms will be just as you left them, but you'll have changed – the physical and mental effort of the climb will have seen to that – while the cliff will still be as dark and as wild as ever, untamed by your passage.

I lost my fear of Fairhead as soon as I started leading climbs there, and I even became possessive of the place once I started putting up new routes of my own. Now that I was familiar with its grey expanses, I could flirt with its fierceness without being overwhelmed. There was never any shortage of virgin rock for us to explore, and we had it more or less to ourselves for decades. Following the end of the Troubles in the late 1990s, there was a slow increase in visitors from Britain, but the cliff never became crowded, and few others shared our passion for new routing.

We put up scores of high-quality new climbs over the decades – so many that we even lost track of one of mine. All new routes are precious, but this one, climbed in 1991, was doubly so as it was an E4 – my hardest route to date. It was mistakenly left out of the next edition of the guidebook, edited by us, and we were so busy with work and family that I didn't notice the omission. I forgot about the climb until I came across the details of it in my diary twenty-five years later. I was able to trace the faulty record keeping but of the route itself there was no sign.

It was in the wild heart of the crag, and when I went looking for it I couldn't pin down its exact location – it was one crack line among dozens. Heather and grass would have sprouted again in its grooves, along with the odd dandelion and bobbing harebell, and generations of woodlice would have lived undisturbed in its cobwebby cracks. The brushed-off, dirt-free line of ascent would have long since reverted to the anonymity of the unclimbed rock on either side and may even have been re-cleaned and climbed by someone else as a presumed first ascent. But I can't complain. For nigh on fifty years Calvin and I have dipped together into the treasure trove of unclimbed rock at Fairhead and have never come away empty-handed.

We cleaned new lines when it was too wet to climb. The cliff was so high that scanning the rock from above or below only revealed so much, and it always took an abseil down the face before you could judge whether a possible line might 'go'. Then the hours and days of hard work would begin: hanging on the rope and digging muck and loose rock out of the cracks and brushing little edges clean until, after the final dust-off, the pioneering climbing effort could begin.

We arrived up one Saturday morning in 2007 to a low sky and heavy rain. The nearest road to the crag comes to a dead end near the last few farms on the headland, leaving a ten-minute walk to the clifftop. You pass a small lake, Lough Doo, the Black Lake, just before reaching the cliff edge, and there, where a stream flows out of the lake, is the Ballycastle Descent Gully – the climbers' pathway to the bottom of the cliff.

We parked near a gate and waited for a break in the weather. When that didn't come, Calvin got ready to go prospecting, but I was happy to stay and read the paper. I knew what it would be like over at the crag - the soaking heather, the wind blowing the rope back up from the edge, the fingers freezing as you tied knots for the abseil. Once over the top and sliding slowly down the rock face, you'd be out of the worst of the wind. As the wet rope moved jerkily through the friction device on your harness, you'd become immersed in your task and oblivious to the mucky water that sprayed out onto your rain jacket. With hood pulled tight, goggles down over your eyes and fingers warming inside your gloves, you'd peer out, a deep-sea diver in an expanse of grey. You could concentrate happily on your chosen strip of soaking-wet rock, and whole hours would slip by as you teased little pebbles out of tapering cracks and used an old ice axe to lever unstable boulders off ledges.

I thought I might go over later, if the rain stopped. But it didn't stop, and I was running out of newspaper when I heard a strange noise, a sort of strangled sound that I took to be from a farm animal. Looking out the rain-dripped window, I saw Calvin standing a few metres away, at the far side of the gate. He was croaking unintelligibly and could neither open the gate nor climb over it.

When he had finished abseiling, he'd made his way along the bottom of the cliff to the gully. A little path picks its way up and around rock steps and shares the space with the stream as it nears the top. That day, there was water flowing everywhere as he plodded uphill, his head low in the heavy rain and his mind on the route he had just cleaned. Suddenly he slipped and tumbled backwards, head first.

He threw his hands out to slow himself but kept falling, bumping over little bluffs as he went. He was conscious of the old ice axe stuck into the harness at his waist – a sharp and efficient cleaning tool that could do him a lot of damage. Then he became airborne over the final 10-metre cliff and crashed onto the grass and heather down below.

He sat up and took stock. He guessed that he had cracked some ribs and that one of his thumbs had suffered damage. He tried to lift the thumb to check it out but found that his shoulder wouldn't work. He made his way slowly back up the gully and lurched over the rough ground towards the road. By the time he got to the gate he was suffering from shock and ready to collapse.

At the hospital in Coleraine he was told he had broken ribs and a dislocated shoulder, and when he was released the next day, strapped up, it was with the warning that he might need surgery. It could have been much worse. He never wore a helmet except in the Alps but on that one occasion he had borrowed mine, to keep the rain off.

When you take a big fall, the overwhelming sense is not of fear but of information being processed at top speed. Your conscious self lags behind as your brain takes in a burst of detail: the rushing air; the knee, arm or hip hitting the rock; the sound of something cracking. Then, just as the mind begins to sort out the facts, the pain comes rushing in and the shock explodes.

The following weekend was our first weekend at home in three months. It was early July – the middle of the climbing season – and while Calvin was trussed up in a sling with weeks of physiotherapy ahead of him, I sought out other people to climb with.

But then I had a mishap too. I was in Dalkey Quarry one evening and had climbed a short steep route that was a well-known test piece. I sat securely anchored at the top of the cliff, just back from the edge, and belayed my partner as he climbed. He was having trouble at the hardest part of the climb, and I gave him what help I could by pulling tight on the rope as he tried the crux moves. 'Jam your left hand in the crack and twist the left foot in. There's nothing for your right foot, just friction on the wall. Then pull up and get a high jam for the right hand, and then that's it, you're over the hard bit. At least that's the way I did it,' I said.

But it didn't work for him, and he slumped back, the tight rope stretching under his weight. He tried a second time and failed again. 'Right,' he said. 'I'll have a rest and then give it one last go.'

I lowered him to a foothold so that he could get his breath back, and then he tried again. I pulled hard on the rope as he lunged for the crucial hand jam, my hands knuckle-white as I dragged in the slack and yanked it through the belay device to secure it. But the tension of the tight rope wasn't enough to help him. He flew off the rock and as his full weight came onto the rope, it snapped tightly over the edge, trapping my hands underneath.

The taut weighted rope crushed my fingers into the rock, and they were so badly gashed that I passed out with the pain – but not until after I'd lowered him to the ground. It was all my own fault: I shouldn't have had my hands in such a vulnerable position, and while the situation could have been a major incident in the wild, it was easily managed in the confines of the quarry. My partner was able to scramble around to the top of the cliff and help with some first aid, and soon I had recovered enough to make my own way down and drive home.

Calvin was watching television when I arrived back, and I was telling him what had happened when one of our sons came into the room. Instinctively I whipped my bandaged hands behind my back. Both of us injured! When would we learn a bit of sense? It was Robert, now a kind and thoughtful art student who would be slow to pass judgement on anyone. Michael and Oscar never questioned our climbing either, but there were times when Calvin and I seemed to be the adolescents of the family.

The following week we both had appointments on the same afternoon at the orthopaedic clinic in Loughlinstown hospital. It turned out that I had fractured four of my fingers, and they were never quite the same after. They set a bit unevenly, and while I was back climbing within a few months I couldn't fit them into thin cracks anymore. The knobbly knuckles that come with age didn't help either. Calvin had to adjust too. For months he carried his rucksack over one shoulder only, whenever we went hill walking. He made a good recovery, but part of his shoulder stayed permanently out of place. He didn't let it affect his climbing.

A few years later, just before Easter in 2011, we began our outdoor season by climbing at Pigeon Rock in the Mournes. Pigeon is an easily accessible cliff above the narrow road that encircles the mountains. As we uncoiled the ropes, the sun came out and glinted off the mica specks in the rough granite. It felt like a blessing to be climbing in a rugged valley after the long months of training on an indoor wall.

Calvin decided to do 'Yellow Brick Road', a route he had put up in 1974. He was on an easy move near the top when, without warning, his foot skidded off some grit on a small hold and he fell. He hit a ledge hard before the rope came tight, and as he swung below his top runner, I saw he wasn't making any attempt to climb back up. *Oh dear, he must have banged his ankle – there goes our Easter trip to France*, I thought, and I'd only just booked the ferry the day before. He shouted to me to lower him down, and as he came closer, feet first, I was horrified. There was no blood, but a bone was sticking out of his bare ankle just above the top of his rock shoe.

There were a few other climbers within shouting distance, and they came to help. Maybe we could all carry him down to the road? It was only ten minutes away. But then we saw the rest of the damage. Both ankles were badly broken. He was lifted off by helicopter a few hours later, and over the following week he had two operations that the surgeons said went well. But what did that mean? He would now have permanent metal plates and screws in his ankles, and the hospital's idea of a successful recovery mightn't be the same as ours.

Back to the orthopaedic clinic in Loughlinstown, another queue of plastic chairs and another consultant. This one wore a dicky bow and looked to be near retirement. 'And you do some rock climbing, Mr Torrans?' he asked as he glanced at the notes the nurse had handed him.

'Yes,' said Calvin.

'He does a lot actually,' I butted in, 'and he's very good.' I couldn't have this man thinking he was dealing with a sixty-seven-year-old retiree who did the odd bit of hill walking.

The consultant ignored me anyway. 'Well, Mr Torrans, you won't be doing any more of that.'

No! No! Don't say that, I shouted silently.

The consultant couldn't know what it would mean to us if Calvin was never able to climb again, but to say it so casually, with that condescending smile of his, and that dicky bow. *Bastard*. He went on to talk about how long it would take to recover from the surgery and about the physiotherapy appointments and the months in a wheelchair, and then the weeks on crutches, if all went well.

I stared out past him to where an ambulance was idling in the sunny car park. Calvin could never climb again? He himself seemed unperturbed and didn't ask any questions. I hoped he was still listening because I couldn't take anything in. Would he even be able to walk properly again? I was afraid to ask.

The community nurse in Bray was much more reassuring when she called to our house to talk about ramps, shower stools and commodes. 'You don't have to worry,' she said to me as I saw her to the door. 'He will get better. It's the old people who don't recover.' It was a relief to hear that, and a novelty to have Calvin placed in a younger demographic for a change. Many of the climbers we were mixing with now were young enough to be our grandchildren.

Calvin did his physiotherapy exercises religiously and added more of his own. I'd come home from school to find him in his wheelchair lifting weights. His legs would be straight out and immobilised in their supports, as usual, but he would be working to keep his arms and shoulders strong. One day he couldn't keep the smile off his face. He was stretched out on the floor and was strengthening each ankle in turn with the help of a Theraband. For the first time since the accident he was able to put pressure on his toes and he could see the muscles working. Both legs had become wasted and the tendons stood out from the bones, but now he could start building the muscles up again. Getting his body back under his control took all of his focus.

I waited until he was clearly on the mend before asking him about the accident. Why had he fallen so far, and how had he done so much damage? His reply was casual. The length of the fall was just due to rope stretch, and so-and-so from the Glenfoffany Club had fallen in the exact same spot years ago and had smashed both of his ankles too. As for the consultant, Calvin said that arrogant bastards like that never bothered him and that at no stage, ever, did he think this would affect his climbing. None of those thoughts had even come into his head.

By the end of July he was strong enough to use crutches instead of the wheelchair, and when we went to France in August he shuffled his way to the foot of various crags so that he could belay me while I climbed. Two months later, he was back climbing himself, at Fairhead. Then he got the alpine guidebooks down from the shelf and began making plans for the following summer. I had my partner back: back to share the thrill of climbing and to walk with me again in wild places.

Glossary of climbing terms

abseil descending by making a controlled slide down a rope

arête a narrow ridge of rock or snow

aid gear pulled on for upward progress

belay (n.) an anchor point; (v.) to safeguard a partner by means of a rope running through a friction device

bergschrund the big crevasse that forms where a glacier and rock face meet.

bivouac/bivy a night spent in the open without a tent

col a saddle between two rises

couloir a gully

crux the hardest part of a climb

laybacking a technique used to climb a crack

line an actual or potential climb

peg a metal spike hammered into a thin crack

pitch or rope length the distance to be climbed between two anchor points

protection a piece of equipment jammed or fixed into rock or ice

put up a climb do the first ascent

runner a closed loop that connects the climber's rope to protection by means of karabiners

swinging leads taking turns to lead

téléphérique a cable car

top-roping climbing with the security of a rope running through an anchor point above

About the Author

Clare Sheridan has been at the forefront of Irish climbing for decades and has long been a role model for women climbers. In 2014 she was the first woman to be awarded the Lynam medal by Mountaineering Ireland, and the *Irish Times* said, 'She is to Irish mountaineering what Sonia O'Sullivan is to athletics and Katie Taylor is to boxing.' Clare has written many articles for the *Irish Mountain Log* and co-edited numerous rock climbing guidebooks with her husband, climbing legend Calvin Torrans. She and Calvin have three sons. She is a retired primary school teacher and when she's not away climbing, home is Bray, County Wicklow.

Printed in Great Britain
by Amazon

56412143R00125